Managing Difficult People
In A Week

David Cotton

The Teach Yourself series has been trusted around the world for
over sixty years. This new series of 'In a Week' business books
is des͏   nd the world to
                                                   s learn in

David Cotton is an independent leadership and management trainer, with experience of working in four continents and around 40 countries. His client portfolio reads like a 'Who's Who' of major organizations in local and national government and nearly every industry sector. He spent more than 20 years with two of the 'Big 4' professional service firms before setting up his own training consultancy. He has written 11 books, two of which won publishers' bestseller awards, scores of journal articles and a double award-winning e-learning package on electronic marketplaces. David believes that any manager can learn to prevent and manage difficult behaviours in the workplace if they step back occasionally from their day-to-day duties, reflect on their own behaviours, observe their staff closely and create a motivating environment in which people can work, with support, to the best of their ability. He has written this book to help you to get the best out of yourself and your team, so that you can spend your working time as enjoyably and productively as possible.

Acknowledgements

Thanks to Jane, Philippa and Victoria Cotton for love and support. Thanks to Clare Forrest (*www.structuredlearning.com*) for invaluable advice. Thanks to all my difficult colleagues, bosses, team members and clients for making this book possible!

Teach® Yourself

Managing difficult people

David Cotton

www.inaweek.co.uk

First published in Great Britain in 2014 by Hodder & Stoughton. An Hachette UK company.

First published in US in 2014 by The McGraw-Hill Companies, Inc.

This edition published 2014

British Library Cataloguing in Publication Data: a catalogue record for this title is available from the British Library.

Library of Congress Catalog Card Number: on file.

10 9 8 7 6 5 4 3 2 1

Typeset by Cenveo® Publisher Services.

Printed and bound in Great Britain by CPI Group (UK) Ltd., Croydon, CR0 4YY.

Hodder & Stoughton policy is to use papers that are natural, renewable and recyclable products and made from wood grown in sustainable forests. The logging and manufacturing processes are expected to conform to the environmental regulations of the country of origin.

Hodder & Stoughton Ltd

338 Euston Road

London NW1 3BH

www.hodder.co.uk

Contents

Introduction

Wouldn't it be wonderful if everyone thought and behaved as we do? Working life would be so simple if we could rely on others to behave exactly like us. So often, when someone is out of step with us we brand them 'difficult' when perhaps we mean that their behaviours just don't match our own. Part of the art of dealing with difficult people is to take a step back and examine whether their behaviour is likely to cause any problems for us or others at work, or whether they simply have a different view of life and their apparently 'difficult' behaviour is in no way detrimental to team relationships and productivity. It's when their different approach gets in the way that we have to take action.

This book focuses on two aspects of managing difficult people at work:

● Prevention – creating an environment in which staff feel supported and motivated
● Cure – dealing with difficult behaviour when it arises

Through seven themed chapters, you'll learn a wealth of techniques to manage difficult people at work.

On our first day, Sunday, we'll start to explore the reasons why people may display difficult behaviours at work and the first steps we can take to prevent those behaviours.

On Monday, we'll delve deeper and start to create a toolkit of skills to help in managing difficult people, starting with your own responses to others' behaviour, building rapport, looking at where you have influence as a manager and how to use that influence, developing the most useful and perhaps overlooked skill – listening to other people, being attentive, and asking great questions so that you get quickly to the heart of a matter.

On Tuesday, we'll develop the toolkit and look at more advanced skills, including the ways in which you can use language to influence behaviour, how to trigger useful and appropriate emotional states and behaviours in others, calming angry team members, drawing out quieter people, defending yourself when under attack, and saying 'no' when you mean no.

On Wednesday, we'll drill down to more specific types of difficult behaviour and how to deal with them, including the person who drains the energy from the team, the perpetual complainer, the aggressive person and the team member who abuses privilege.

Thursday is devoted to giving feedback that works and having critical conversations with your staff. Rather than seeing feedback as 'positive' or 'negative', we focus more on feedback as information, and how we can structure that information so that the recipient is left in no doubt about the effects of their behaviours and the need to remedy them.

No matter how hard we try to create harmony at work, we will sometimes encounter conflict, and Friday is entirely devoted to the management of conflict – how it arises, how to defuse tense situations, how to deal with bullying at work, managing power games and then looking at some classic, well-tried models of conflict resolution which are easily applied at work.

Finally, on Saturday, we recognize that sometimes you will need support from others and we'll look at managing persistently difficult behaviour, escalating issues which don't want to go away, the stages in disciplinary proceedings and what to do if you have to take an issue to a more formal disciplinary level.

SUNDAY

Understanding and preventing difficult behaviour

Just as preventive medicine is preferable to curative medicine, so it is better to understand the likely causes of difficult behaviour and prevent it arising than to have to manage difficult behaviours. In this chapter we'll focus on understanding the root causes of difficult behaviour and finding ways to create a stimulating and motivating atmosphere at work to minimize the likelihood of difficult behaviour. When people are happy and motivated at work, they tend to display less 'difficult' behaviour, are easier to manage and are a good deal more productive.

Let's start by looking at some common causes of difficult behaviour and see what we can do to prevent, reduce or remove them.

Motivating the team

There are almost as many theories about what motivates us as there are demotivated people! Here are some examples of motivators and what we can do to create and maintain them:

Motivator As team members we tend to be motivated when we...	Your management role
Enjoy the work	Offer the widest variety of work possible, ensuring that it stretches and develops staff. Avoid favouritism and spread interesting and challenging work evenly across your team, conscious of the need to develop staff rather than simply delegating work to those whom you know are already competent to do it
Like our colleagues	You may have no choice of team members but good management will draw out the best in people. Much of this book will help you to do just that!
Feel that we can approach our manager if we have concerns	Ensure that the 'open door' policy is about mindset as much as the placement of office furniture... Take time to manage: whilst this seems an obvious statement, many managers are too busy 'doing' to manage their teams. If staff members believe that you will judge them if they open up to you, they will bottle up their concerns or share them with each other and you will be left out of the loop.
Like the atmosphere and environment at work	Be positive and encouraging; manage by wandering about and dealing with personal issues as they arise, rather than letting them escalate. Create occasional social activities; allow people some social time within work – it oils the wheels of working relationships and helps the team to become more focused and productive. Do what you can to ensure that the office is clean and tidy, furniture is reasonably comfortable, you have as much natural light as possible and the heating/air conditioning is functioning properly.

Understand the context/ purpose of our work	Take the time to discuss why a particular piece of work is necessary and important, how it links to other pieces of work before/after it and the outputs and outcomes that you are looking for. Give your staff members the opportunity to ask questions and don't make them feel stupid when they don't understand something. It may be that you didn't explain it clearly or establish sufficient context for understanding.
Have reasonable licence to think and act for ourselves	Gauge the strengths of your team members and allow the freedom to act within the bounds of what's safe and possible. Be flexible: just because someone tackled a piece of work differently from the way you might have done it doesn't mean their approach was wrong. See what you can learn from a variety of approaches and be prepared to accept that your way may only be one way. Monitor without interference.
Feel that the reward system is fair and transparent	Treat people fairly, showing no overt favouritism (even if, inevitably, you feel some). This fairness must extend to all aspects of your management.
Know that, if something goes wrong, we will be supported by our colleagues and manager	Be there, be supportive, show you care, protect your team members and deal with things internally wherever you can. Be visible without being too obtrusive. Sometimes the manager's role is like that of a waiter in a restaurant – always there when needed but not getting too close to spoil the enjoyment of the meal.
Feel a reasonable degree of job security	You can't guarantee this, but the better motivated and productive your team members, the greater the likelihood of their and your survival in the organization.

Motivator As team members we tend to be motivated when we...	Your management role
Feel trusted	Don't micro-manage. Let people have space to think for themselves and, where possible, give them sufficient time so that they find solutions to their own problems without your apparent interference. The recruitment process is expensive and time-consuming and we tend to believe that we have recruited the right person to each job. Let them prove that this is the case by trusting them to do their job well.
Feel that they are in the right role	Sometimes, we put the wrong person in a particular role. As managers we should be humble enough to admit to ourselves when we make a mistake and sensitive to others' feelings if we need to move them into a different role.
Learn on the job	Ensure that after each assignment there is a thorough debrief. This serves two purposes – to learn from what worked and embed it in future best practice and to understand how and where things went wrong so that the same mistakes cannot be repeated. This is not about blame but about understanding how something could have happened and implementing sufficient controls and systems to prevent its recurrence without becoming too draconian and limiting freedom to act. Flex your management style according to situation. A single management style will only work part of the time. Management styles are often described as: • Directive (telling people what to do) • Affiliative (treating your staff as you would treat your friends) • Participative (democratic and consensus-seeking) • Coaching (asking good questions to help staff to find their own solutions) • Visionary (painting a word picture of how things could be to inspire others to work towards it) • Pacesetting (leading by example and demonstrating how to do something so others can copy the method)

Feel that we are in the job we best deserve	A big cause of difficult behaviour at work is envy or resentment of others (and this may include envy of you and your position). It tends to happen when some team members are perceived to be given unfair advantages, opportunities or promotions or a team member believes that they should have had the promotion which you received. You can do little about the latter other than treat them fairly and respectfully and give them good, challenging and stimulating work. You can do a great deal about the former ensuring that as far as it is within your gift, you are scrupulously fair in your objective setting, appraisal and rating and recommendations for advancement.
Feel that we are recognized for the quality of our work and achievements	Recognition of good work costs nothing and can be highly motivating. Be sure to tell people when they have done a good job. Keep it in proportion to the size and complexity of the task and balance private and public recognition.
Feel that our manager knows us as people and not simply as members of the workforce	Get to know your staff as people and respect them as the 'whole being' who comes to work rather than only as a person fulfilling a particular work role. Take time to discover what interests them outside work and learn as much as you can about them, without being intrusive. As you get to know them so you will deepen the relationship and, often, your respect for them.

A lack of motivation is a prime cause of difficult behaviour and is, for the most part, preventable. There are many other things that you can do as a manager to prevent difficulties arising.

Driving up team performance

It's said that teams go through several stages in their evolution – forming (when they first come together), storming (when members jockey for position), norming (when they settle into their appointed roles) and performing (when they do what we originally planned for them!). In reality there are other stages – if the same team is left together for too long, doing the same work, things become stale and the team enters a 'dorming' (complacent, bored, sleeping-on-the-job) stage. At this point we'll start to see lots of difficult behaviour as members lose their drive and motivation to work. We need to anticipate this stage and take preventive measures to drive up team performance and maintain people's enthusiasm for their work. Preventive measures are designed to send the team back through the forming, storming and norming loop, which refreshes the team and drives it back up to great performance:

- Job rotation
- Secondments (as you move someone out of the team temporarily, roles are reallocated)
- More stretching assignments and objectives
- New roles and responsibilities
- New person in the team

Almost anything you do which changes the focus or structure of the team will have the effect of revitalizing ('reforming') the team and whilst you may have to suffer temporary grumbles from those who dislike change, the longer term effects are good for team performance and minimize difficult behaviours.

Summary

Western medicine has traditionally focused on curing people who are unwell. Eastern medicine has traditionally focused on keeping people well so that they don't become ill. Inevitably you will meet difficult people at work and the more you can do to create an upbeat motivating atmosphere the fewer difficult people you will encounter. Prevention is better than cure.

Be fair and transparent in your actions, set aside real time to manage and help people to understand the context for their work. Let them exercise some freedom to act and help them to develop within the bounds of their jobs. See your team members as individuals rather than as an amorphous blob of workers and they will feel more valued. Show that you notice when they work particularly hard and recognize their achievements. Everything you do to support the team will help you to reduce difficult behaviours and allow you more time to develop your own management skills.

SUNDAY

MONDAY

TUESDAY

WEDNESDAY

THURSDAY

FRIDAY

SATURDAY

Fact-check (answers at the back)

1 Preventing difficult behaviour is:
a) Better than curing it afterwards ❏
b) As useful as curing it afterwards ❏
c) Neither better nor worse than curing it afterwards ❏
d) Not possible ❏

2 Staff will be more motivated:
a) When they like their colleagues, even though the work is not enjoyable ❏
b) When the work is enjoyable, even if they don't like their colleagues ❏
c) When the work is enjoyable and they like their colleagues ❏
d) Whether or not they enjoy the work or like their colleagues ❏

3 An 'open door' policy means:
a) The door to the manager's office is always open ❏
b) Working in an open plan office ❏
c) Staff must knock before entering the manager's office ❏
d) The manager is approachable when staff have concerns ❏

4 When someone doesn't understand something, the manager should:
a) Berate them for their stupidity ❏
b) Give them time to ask questions and not make them feel stupid for doing so ❏
c) Tell them to go and think about it and come back when they have understood it ❏
d) Delegate the work to someone else ❏

5 When a manager delegates a piece of work, the team member should:
a) Do it the way the manager would do it ❏
b) Have some freedom to do it their own way ❏
c) Follow the rules to the letter ❏
d) Expect to be told precisely how to do it ❏

6 To drive up team performance you could:
a) Rotate jobs, give more stretching assignments or send people on secondments ❏
b) Set team members unachievable goals ❏
c) Push people much harder ❏
d) Sack the team members and hire replacements ❏

7 Recognizing good work:
a) Is not necessary. Salary should be reward enough ❏
b) Is generally viewed as patronizing behaviour ❏
c) Can be a real motivator ❏
d) Is too 'pink and fluffy' and not recommended ❏

8 The purpose of a debrief is to:
a) Find out who is to blame for everything that went wrong ❏
b) Celebrate the end of an assignment ❏
c) Help a manager to rate people against their objectives ❏
d) Learn from what went well and to prevent recurrence of anything that went wrong ❏

9 When you delegate a piece of work:
a) It should be done your way, which is the only guarantee of success ❑
b) It's fine that someone does it their way – you might learn from it ❑
c) You should set out the method in detail and tolerate no deviation from it ❑
d) It's best that you intervene as often as possible to ensure that it is done correctly ❑

10 Social time at work:
a) Should be frowned upon because it hampers productivity ❑
b) Should take up the bulk of the working day ❑
c) Should be banned entirely ❑
d) Oils the wheels of working relationships ❑

MONDAY

Developing skills for managing difficult people

When our team members and workmates are difficult, it's all too easy to take things personally. Our primitive reactions tell us to fight, flee or freeze – to counter bad behaviour with what, at a professional level may be viewed as equally bad behaviour; to bury our heads, ostrich-like, in the sand and do nothing, or even walk away from the problem; or to be caught off guard and genuinely not know the best action to take.

- Rule number one in dealing with difficult people: *this isn't about you.*
- Rule number two: *actually, it may be about you,* but you have to deal with it dispassionately, setting your emotions to one side and deal with it as though rule number one is true.

Whether rule one or rule two applies, it's worth taking a step back and asking if there is anything in your own behaviour which may have prompted the perceived difficult behaviour in the other person. If so, it becomes easier to manage: acknowledge and amend your behaviour. If you can genuinely see nothing in your own behaviour which could have prompted difficult behaviour from someone else, then resist the urge to take anything personally and do your best to investigate the underlying causes of the issue and deal with them at an objective, rational level.

Today we are going to look at essential skills for managing difficult people.

Where we have a strong relationship – real rapport – with our team members, we should encounter fewer issues.

Building rapport at individual and team level

The word *rapport* comes from the French word *rapporter*, meaning 'to relate'. When we relate to people at anything more than a superficial level, we send out signals to them to say 'I'm just like you' and we receive similar signals from them. We like people who are similar to us and who appear to like us. Two people who are naturally in rapport tend to mimic aspects of each other's body language, so one of the easiest ways to send out rapport-building signals is to do just that – notice how the other person sits, stands or speaks and copy them. So, for example, if the other person crosses their legs or folds their arms, do the same. If they speak quickly, speak quickly back to them.

This is all very well as long as they don't become conscious that you are you copying them: if they do, it will instantly break rapport. Now we have a dilemma – we know that copying creates rapport and we know that if they notice, it will break rapport, but we still want to do it at some level because it works. What's the solution? The answer is to do what they do on a smaller or bigger scale rather than exactly as they did it. If they fold their arms, cross your wrists; if they cross their ankles, cross your legs. A scaled up or down version of their gestures sends the same signals at a subconscious level as an identical gesture, but you don't risk them noticing that you are copying them.

You can mirror other aspects of communication – speed of speech, inflection of voice, smiles, arm and hand gestures. A more profound way to establish rapport, although more difficult to achieve, is breathing in time with the other person. Primates, after love-making, tend to breathe in synch with each other for some time afterwards. If, as a by-product of the most intimate act between two people, we breathe in time with each other, then it's reasonable to assume that synchronized breathing will create that sense of closeness. Watch the other person's shoulders rise and fall with each breath. Note, too, that when someone is talking they must be breathing out, so breathe out with them. When they have used up their breath in speaking for a while, they have to inhale again to continue, so breathe in with them. It takes little time to establish a pattern, but do avoid synchronizing with anyone whose body size is vastly different from yours or who suffers from any respiratory problems!

Watch two friends in a public place. They will mirror each other's body language quite naturally. It's interesting to note that if one always leads and the other follows, the first is seen by both as the dominant one in the relationship. If the leading and following is evenly spread, then they see each other as equals in the relationship. Try mirroring someone's body language for a while and then change yours. If they change theirs to match yours at this point you will have the influence – the upper hand – and they will tend to be influenced by whatever you say next. Be alert to those moments.

Mirroring a single person's body language is relatively easy. You can't, of course, do the same with an entire team. You can, however, mirror the person who is speaking at any one time, or the person you are addressing. This way makes everyone feel included and warmer towards you. It also has the effect of making you really start to observe people and pay attention to them, which will help you to build better and closer relationships with them.

Understanding your spheres of influence and how to use them

In any situation, it's worth considering:

- What can I control (or be in control of)?
- Who or what can I influence?
- What is beyond my influence and control?

Think of it as:

Control
Influence
Nothing

Start with control. Is there any part of this situation in which I can take some control? Yes? Do it! No? Move on. Is there anyone or anything I can influence? Yes? Do it! No? Move on. Everything else belongs in the *Nothing* box. There's nothing you can do there and any attempts to do anything are a waste of emotional and physical energy.

So often we find ourselves worrying about things which are outside our sphere of control and influence, instead of applying our energy to worthwhile things in areas where we can make a difference.

Imagine that you have a bank account in which you can deposit something we'll call *positive emotional energy*. Every time something nice happens during the day you can make a deposit in your bank account and the account can grow so that you feel even happier by the end of the day than you did in the morning. Each time something unpleasant happens, of course, you can remove *positive emotional energy* from the account.

One morning, you wake up to realize that the alarm clock has not sounded and you are late. The toaster burns breakfast, the children won't get ready for school, the car won't start at first and when it does, you soon get stuck in a traffic jam. Each incident is relatively trivial but depletes the stock in your bank account. The cumulative effect is wearing you down. You arrive at work and follow your usual ritual of greeting certain people on the way to your desk. The first person responds to your 'Good morning', as does the second. So far, so good. But the third is deeply engrossed in a piece of work and doesn't reply. Well that's it! That person has single-handedly ruined your day and now you're angry!

Take a step back – everything that has happened so far is, in the great scheme of things, utterly trivial, and you've allowed the angst to accumulate. The one thing that you can control is your behaviour, and it's unfair to treat others badly simply because your day didn't start well. Put everything in perspective. You have a home, a job and a full stomach. There's little to complain about!

TIP *I was recently driving along a British motorway to visit a client when the traffic came to a standstill. According to the local radio station, the traffic jam was due to an accident 50km further along the motorway. The debris would apparently take an hour to clear. I called my client and explained that I would be a little late, then put on some music and started to drift off to sleep, thinking that when it was time to move, the driver behind would sound his horn. As I began to doze I was woken by someone screeching outside. I looked out and saw a man standing on the wheel arch of his 4-wheel drive, shouting at 50km of traffic to move out of his way because he was in a hurry. Now that's a man who has seriously misfiled the traffic jam in a box called 'Control'. The one thing he could control was his behaviour – one of the few areas of life in which we have some choice.*

As a manager, everything that you do and say gives your team the permission to do and say the same things. You can't flip a switch and be a manager when you choose and switch off when you don't feel like it. If you are rude and bad-tempered, it gives your team permission to be the same. When they ape your behaviour, you forfeit the right to complain about it. As a role model, you need to learn self-discipline and to act rationally based on what's in your sphere of control and influence. The one thing which you can absolutely control is your own behaviour. Very often, when managers complain that they have a difficult team member, the team member is doing nothing more than copying the manager's own behaviour. Hold up a mirror to yourself and ask whether you are the role model that you should be for your team. Then start making some seriously big deposits of positive emotional energy in your account, and reflect on when it's useful to make withdrawals from the account.

Listening skills

Active listening

One of the least developed skills in most of us is listening, yet the greatest sign of respect that you can show another human being is to listen – really listen – to them. We speak on average at around 150 words per minute and we can understand our own language perfectly spoken at up to 600 words per minute. This means that for a large proportion of the time when someone else is talking to us, our conscious mind has nothing to do. So, we either drift away on a short mental holiday (not listen) or say what we want to say (interrupt) because the brain has spare capacity.

Good listening takes practice. Try turning on a radio talk show and listening with rapt attention for five full minutes, without doing anything else at all, then see how much you can recall of what you've just heard. Now that's *passive* listening – listening without doing anything – and that's not the best way to listen to others in face-to-face or telephone conversation. *Active* listening is about engaging with the other person, through good questions, summary of key ideas and clarification of what you've heard. Avoid saying 'So what you're trying to say is...' because the other person knows full well what they were trying to say: they've just said it. Instead, turn the conversation round and say, for example, 'Let me check my understanding of that...' and then paraphrase what they said.

Listening without assumptions

Our brains are wonderful. Given half a story, our brains will cheerfully supply the other half. We don't like things which are incomplete, so we flesh out stories based on scant information. If we assume something to be true, based on that sparse information, we will then act as though it is true. Imagine that you have inherited a team from another manager. You were warned as you took over that Fred is a really difficult character and you need to be careful in your dealings with him. Armed with this titbit of information, you meet Fred for the first time and are immediately struck by his bad behaviour. What a good thing your colleague forewarned you. In reality, Fred may be a pussycat, and the outgoing manager may have generalized based on a single incident or simply felt that the chemistry was somehow wrong between him and Fred. It may, of course, be the outgoing manager who was a difficult person. If you believe that Fred is going to be difficult, then your brain will filter in any shred of evidence that this is so, and filter out anything which contradicts this basic premise. Poor Fred doesn't stand a chance. Each time you see him, you imagine the label you've hung above his head saying 'difficult person' and he will have to do a great deal to disabuse you of this notion.

Good managers set aside any preconceived notions about their staff, spend time getting to know and understand them and then flex their management style according to the needs and subjective experience of the staff member. Anything else is an injustice to the person in front of you.

TIP *When I first starting working for a large professional services firm I was constantly given pen portraits of clients whom I was visiting for the first time. Some were described as delightful, others as really difficult. After a while, I asked my colleagues not to tell me anything about our clients other than the services which we had offered, so that I could form my own judgements. I would return from a client to hear a colleague say "Isn't X horrible?" and "I don't envy you working with Y", and yet I had found both X and Y delightful to work with. Set your assumptions aside and deal with what's in front of you. Any presuppositions about others will become self-fulfilling prophecies as you filter in and out everything which accords with your beliefs about them. And that's not giving anyone a fair chance.*

Attentiveness – permissions and continuations

Technology is wonderful. Using a simple handheld device we can talk to others, see their faces on the screen, send and receive emails and texts and a host of other fun things. And it becomes an obsession. We feel incomplete if we do not have our smart phone in our hand or on the desk in front of us. Even as we talk to others we manage surreptitious glances at the phone to see if we have received a new message. We interrupt one-to-one meetings to take incoming calls, which we would know nothing about had we had the courtesy to switch off the phone and put it away before our meeting began. Imagine that you go to see your boss and just as you begin to think that you have her attention you see her eyes drift towards her mobile phone. There are two big issues here:

- When you talk to your staff, be present. Switch off your phone and put it where you can't see it.
- If you constantly use your phone during meetings, you encourage your staff to do the same. Effectively, everything that you do and say as a manager gives your staff permission to do the same and you forfeit the right to complain about any behaviours in them which you demonstrate. You have to be a role model for them.

Attentiveness – the art of being present – takes practice and becomes increasingly difficult in a world of sound bites, visual imagery and shortening attention spans. Yet it is through attentiveness that you start to pick up on visual and auditory clues which tell you something about how the other person is feeling and allow you to manage them better. Focus, listen, observe and be aware.

Once you start to develop this awareness, then you not only gain more from conversation but can exercise gentle controls to ensure that both you and your team member have the opportunity to speak.

Imagine that you are sitting talking to your team member about a problem. Incline your head slightly to one side to indicate that you are listening. Nod occasionally and ask clarifying questions.

Avoid interrupting the other person because it may suggest that you consider what you have to say to be more important. A simple way to quietly direct the conversation without verbal interruption is to sit with hands clasped and slightly raised up in front of you, as you are listening. When you want to speak, unclasp your hands and lean slightly forward and the other person will generally pick up on the cue that you have something to say. When you have finished, clasp your hands again and sit back a little in your chair. In this way you subtly signal permission to speak. As long as your hands remain clasped you are signalling permission to continue.

Questioning to get to the heart of an issue

We all have favourites: that's just human nature. But displaying favouritism at work is a perfect recipe for causing difficult behaviour in others. We must appear fair-minded and even-handed in our management of others if we are to maintain our credibility. It's difficult to step away from a subjective view of our staff members and deal with them as equals, and it's often in asking questions that we start to display our biases towards and away from our team members.

What we say and what we actually mean may be rather different. For example, many of us will exaggerate for effect, generalize based on something specific, omit information because we assume that the other person knows more than they actually do or slightly twist the truth because it suits our purposes and then believe the fabricated version.

Linguistics, the scientific study of human language, talks of the *surface structure* – the words we actually utter, and the *deep structure* – the real meaning of what we say. Imagine that the surface structure is the surface of the sea and the deep structure is the sea bed:

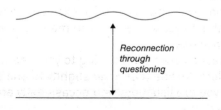

Reconnection through questioning

The art of great questioning is to reconnect the surface (what was said) with the sea bed (what was actually meant). When you are dealing with difficult behaviour you need to work as far as possible with the facts. That's not to discount emotions, which also play a part, but if you can quickly establish the facts you have something more tangible to work with.

The easiest way to get to the heart of an issue quickly is to listen for three things:

● generalizations
● deletions
● distortions

Each of these is common in speech. It's possible, when you hear any of these surface level statements to reconnect immediately to the deep structure so that you have something to manage. Let's look at each in turn:

Generalizations

Imagine that your team member is complaining to you and says angrily: 'I'm sick to death of the invoice processing system. It has never worked!'

The generalized word in that statement is *never*. Take that single word and inflect it as a question: 'Never?' or if you feel that this is too blunt, ask 'It has *never* worked?'

At this point the team member will pause slightly and then say, for example, 'Well it hasn't worked properly since the upgrade two weeks ago.' Now you have something more concrete to deal with. If someone includes *never*, *always*, *everything*, *everybody*, *nobody* or other generalized words in a dramatic statement turn the word into a question. The effect is to reconnect the surface statement to the actual meaning and now you can have a less emotive, more rational discussion about the underlying causes of the issue. This generalization, often for dramatic effect, is a throwback to childhood when a child will say to a parent 'Can have a new bike? *All* my friends have one. *Everyone* except me has a new bike.' This same childlike behaviour spills over into adult conversation.

Deletions

We cannot say everything that we are thinking because we simply don't have time! Imagine asking a colleague: 'Are you comfortable sitting on that part-metallic, part-fabric structure which sits around 90 cm off the floor, is supported by a bent aluminium fabric and offers dorsal support through an adjustable rigid, fabric-covered back plate?' It's rather simpler to say 'chair'. We speak in shorthand and for the most part we understand that shorthand. At times, we need to get beyond the surface structure deletion to the underlying deeper meaning so that we have something to manage. For example, your team member says 'I just don't feel that I am getting enough support here.' The word *support* omits vital information. If you are to give the person sufficient support you need to know more precisely what they believe is missing. Ask 'What kind of support *specifically* do you need?'

Whenever you become aware of a deletion, ask *who, what, where, when, how* **specifically**? Instantly the other person will reconnect and tell you precisely what they want. You may notice that we have not included the word *why* in this list of question words. *Why* often provokes a defensive response and may be better avoided. Soften a *why?* question with *what* or *how*.

Distortions

A distortion is a false linking of two ideas. Typically someone will suggest that X causes Y when in reality the two are not connected. In this case, we need to construct a question which unravels the false connection in the speaker's mind and gets us back to something factual and more manageable.

For example, your team member may say 'You don't like me any more. You don't give me praise.' The false connection here is between liking and praising. To disconnect the two you could ask 'How does my not praising you suggest that I don't like you?' or 'Does everyone who likes you praise you?'

Whenever you are dealing with difficult behaviour, do your best to get to the facts as gently and as quickly as you can. Listen for generalizations, deletions and distortions and ask a single question in each case which instantly reconnects the statement uttered to the meaning of that statement or the

SUNDAY

MONDAY

TUESDAY

WEDNESDAY

THURSDAY

FRIDAY

SATURDAY

facts which sit beneath the surface. It's a great discipline: it makes you listen and focus and displays a rational, fair-minded approach to the other person.

It's this objective, fair-mindedness that we will explore next.

Being objective and fair

Separating facts from emotions

Listen to a factual radio broadcast for five minutes and note on a piece of paper each time the reporter strays from facts to supposition to emotive statements. We are not good at sticking to facts because the facts alone may not support our argument. We make assumptions, suppose things to be true which may not be supported by facts and throw in our own feelings for good measure. In managing difficult people we need to distinguish between facts and 'fillers' – the padding of statements and arguments for effect and to strengthen a particular case. Only then can we manage objectively and fairly. If a staff member is crying about an incident, it's unlikely that you will get a clear statement of facts from them, but you need the facts if you are to manage an issue effectively. It's easy to be swayed by someone in a highly emotional state to believe that they have right on their side. It's equally easy for some people to display high emotion in order to win others over. Look beyond the emotions, be calm, ask good questions and listen for factual content.

Distinguishing between the person and the issue

A key principle in dealing with difficult people is to separate the person from the issue. We can attack the behaviour but we must not attack the person. So we would never say 'I really dislike you' but could say 'I really dislike this type of behaviour.' No matter how personal the issue feels to you, it's imperative that you set those feelings aside and deal as objectively as you can with the behaviour itself. We can change our behaviours but we cannot change the person we are, and it's almost impossible to re-establish a good working relationship after a blistering personal attack. The moment you start to attack the person you become over-emotional and you lose credibility as you display a lack of control. If you treat the behaviour almost as an object, you set aside your emotions and become more dispassionate, credibility is preserved and you will be afforded more respect.

The fine balance between aggressive and assertive management

Most of us tend to behave in a combination of three ways – aggressively, assertively and submissively. Aggression and submission are two extremes, and the ideal is assertiveness. Some of the traits of each set of behaviours are outlined below. These are indicative of the types of behaviour exhibited. The lists are not exhaustive and most people who favour a particular type of behaviour will not exhibit every characteristic in a specific list. Tick the statements which you honestly believe seem to describe you and add up your totals. The maximum possible for each behavioural type is 14.

SUNDAY
MONDAY
TUESDAY
WEDNESDAY
THURSDAY
FRIDAY
SATURDAY

Aggressive traits			
I am a bully		I will hurt others to satisfy my needs	
I like to feel powerful		I take advantage of people who cannot retaliate	
My actions and words are the right ones		I boast about myself, so people know I am strong, important and clever	
I can be lonely because I drive other people away		Everything that goes wrong is someone else's fault – I look for people to blame	
I have lost friends because I cannot see others as equals		I am very energetic, but I don't harness that energy for positive action	
Deep down, I don't really like myself		I play on submissive people who give in to my bullying behaviour	
I stand very upright		I have a loud voice	
Total			

Submissive traits			
I tend to sacrifice my own needs for other people		I feel insecure and inferior	
I have low self-esteem		I am often very angry at the advantages others take of me and I turn that anger inwards, feeling that there is little point in doing anything about it	
I hide my true feelings		I pretend that everything is OK, although I am constantly anxious	
I withdraw from others because of my inferiority complex		I find compliments difficult to handle	
I lack energy		I am not an overtly enthusiastic person	
I spend no time on my self		I tend to be apologetic	
I stoop		I tend to talk quietly	
Total			

Assertive traits			
I stand up for my own and others' rights		I am not interested in point scoring	
I achieve my goals		I respect other people	

Assertive traits		
I aim for everybody to win	I negotiate and compromise positively	
I am aware of my own feelings	I can explain my feelings to others	
I am trusted because I always keep my promises	I am at peace with myself	
I acknowledge my own success without having to boast about it	I inspire enthusiasm in others	
I have an upright, relaxed posture	I maintain eye contact	
Total		

Understanding behavioural trends in yourself and others

Ask yourself these questions:

- Being absolutely honest with yourself, which set of characteristics describes you most accurately?
- How does that behaviour manifest itself at work? At home? In social situations?
- What would you have to do to change a particular behaviour in order to become less aggressive, less submissive and more assertive?
- Choose a particular behaviour from the aggressive or submissive lists that you would like to change. What does that behaviour give you that an alternative from the assertive traits list would not give you?
- If you were to change an aspect of your behaviour, what would the new behaviour give you? How would it change your working, family or social relationships?

Now consider the difficult people whom you manage:

- Which characteristics do they particularly display?
- Do they show a particular preference for a specific block of behaviours?

- When there is conflict between two people at work, what are their predominant characteristics? For example, aggressive vs submissive (bullying); aggressive vs aggressive (headlong clash and power struggle).

The better you are able to characterize the behaviours you are seeing, the better placed you are to manage them.

Summary

Whether or not a difficult issue is about you, set aside emotion, assumption and supposition and deal with the facts of the situation. Establish rapport with your team members and notice the improvement in your relationships with them. Rather than agonize about things which are outside your control, focus on those things which you can control and influence. The greatest sign of respect you can show anyone is to listen to them and give them permission and space to say what they need to say. Ask good clarifying questions so that you get to the heart of a matter quickly and really listen to the answers with focus on the issue rather than the person. Be assertive, taking care not to let this spill over into aggression and the fair-mindedness that comes with assertive behaviour will enhance your credibility at work and others' trust in you. Take time out regularly to reflect on your own behaviour and do what you can to ensure that you are the best possible role model for others.

SUNDAY

MONDAY

TUESDAY

WEDNESDAY

THURSDAY

FRIDAY

SATURDAY

Fact-check (answers at the back)

1 One way to show that you are listening is to:
a) Summarize everything the other person says ❑
b) Interrupt the other person ❑
c) Nod vigorously ❑
d) Incline your head ❑

2 We speak, on average, at:
a) 150 words per minute ❑
b) 600 words per minute ❑
c) 350 words per minute ❑
d) 200 words per minute ❑

3 Two people in rapport:
a) Mirror each other's body language ❑
b) Buy each other drinks ❑
c) Avoid eye contact ❑
d) Use very different gestures ❑

4 Our spheres of influence may be categorized as:
a) Contradiction, influence, nothing ❑
b) Connection, influence, nothing ❑
c) Control, influence, nothing ❑
d) Control, inspiration, nothing ❑

5 Sometimes we get angry at work because:
a) We are surrounded by stupid people at work ❑
b) We have allowed the cumulative effect of trivial things to assume disproportionate importance ❑
c) We have allowed the cumulative effect of too little sleep to cloud our rational thinking ❑
d) We have no self-control ❑

6 It is important when listening:
a) To create assumptions based on visual and auditory cues ❑
b) To assume that we know where the other person's conversation is leading us ❑
c) To treat our assumptions as facts ❑
d) To set aside our assumptions ❑

7 Many of us, in conversation, create:
a) Generalizations, deletions and displacements ❑
b) Generalizations, deletions and distortions ❑
c) Generalizations, derivations and distortions ❑
d) Generalizations, disjunctions and distortions ❑

8 Good questions reconnect the:
a) Sky and the ocean bed ❑
b) Shallow structure and deep structure ❑
c) Surface structure and deep structure ❑
d) Surface structure and deep sea ❑

9 In managing difficult behaviour:
a) It's good to become emotional, because it wins people over ❑
b) Make people feel stupid if they become too emotional ❑
c) Put emotions to one side and work with the facts ❑
d) It's fine to work with emotions and facts in equal measure ❑

10 When we hear someone
   generalizing we should:
a) Take what they say at
   face value ❑
b) Tell them not to be silly ❑
c) Encourage them to offer
   further generalizations ❑
d) Use their generalized word
   as a question to get to the
   underlying facts ❑

SUNDAY

MONDAY

TUESDAY

WEDNESDAY

THURSDAY

FRIDAY

SATURDAY

TUESDAY

More advanced skills for managing difficult people

Today we are going to focus on more advanced skills for managing people. We'll look at tricks of language and influence, at how to change people's behaviours in a second, at how to be calm in trying circumstances and how to calm angry people.

Perhaps we think of difficult people as those exhibiting distasteful or unacceptable behaviours, but quiet people who lack the confidence to express themselves can be equally challenging. We'll see how to draw out the quieter people in the group so that they feel they have permission to speak. Sometimes you may feel under attack from others and we'll look at a useful technique for staving off a verbal attack. It can be difficult to say 'no' to others, particularly those in authority and yet we may well feel worse when we say 'yes'. There are many ways to say no without uttering the word 'no'!

The language of influence
Positive versus negative language

The true meaning of a communication is the response which it elicits. It doesn't matter what you intended to say, nor how you intended to say it: what matters is how the other person received it. So we must become acutely aware of our choice of words, our tonality and the accompanying body language. We must put ourselves in the shoes of others and imagine how we look and sound from the outside. Our words and tonality can have a profound effect on others, buoying them up or knocking them down. Others may be upset by a slight edge to our voice which was entirely unintentional.

Part of our job as managers is to influence our team members. It's important that we focus on positive language. Negatives are a trick of language, but we can't experience a negative – we can only talk in negatives. For example, don't think of an elephant right now. Don't imagine one jumping up and down next to you. And it's not a green one. Oh, and while you are not thinking of an elephant, don't for a second imagine slicing off the top of a lemon and don't even consider sucking out the juice. The very act of speaking in negatives implants in others' minds the very image of the thing which we don't want them to focus on. One of the reasons why small children appear to misbehave is because we tell them what not do, thus beautifully implanting in their minds the very image of the thing we don't want them to focus on. Diets fail when we talk to ourselves about what we are not going to eat: 'Today, I'm not going to eat *chocolate...*'

If we want to influence people, we need to develop the ability to use positive language. This means avoiding words like *no, not, never, nothing, didn't, mustn't, can't, shan't, won't* and *haven't*. You'll find it difficult at first, but with practice it becomes easier and easier. Talk in positive terms about the behaviours you expect to see, making no reference to any behaviours that you don't want to see. You will appear more positive, you'll be implanting images of good behaviour in others and you'll be surprised at the positive effect it has on others.

Power words

Whenever you use the word 'but', it tends to erase everything said before it: 'I hear what you are saying, but...' suggests that you are not listening to what someone is saying. 'I do understand what you mean, but...' says that you are not prepared to understand the other person. Try substituting 'and' for 'but'. The other person will be much more prepared to accept what follows the 'and' as an extension of the discussion rather than a rebuttal of what they just said. Even 'I hear what you are saying, and...' is more readily accepted than 'but'.

In a recent study, it was proved that the word 'because' can vastly strengthen even a relatively weak argument. When we were children, adults would justify their arguments with 'because'. It seems that we have been conditioned to accept that a rationale will follow each 'because', so over time we stop listening very hard to the justification and the 'because' almost becomes the justification in its own right. This will tend to work when the stakes are fairly low, but when the stakes are raised, the listener will spend more time weighing up the arguments before giving a response, instead of taking a short-cut and caving in at the mention of 'because'.

Embedded commands

Perhaps the most powerful language technique for influence is embedded commands. Since you were a small child, every time an adult told you to do something, they would downwardly inflect their speech. So 'Sit down' and 'Sit up straight' are each uttered with a downward inflection (the starting notes are higher than the ending notes of the command). Our subconscious becomes attuned to the cadence and knows that it is being commanded to do something. Now we are generally polite people who don't like to sound bossy and can't spend our working lives ordering people around. The embedded command is a way of subtly introducing a command into a longer 'fluffier' sentence. The listener consciously hears the complete sentence and thinks little of it. The listener's subconscious perfectly picks out the embedded command and acts on it, without the listener being aware that they have been commanded to do anything.

There are four simple stages in creating an embedded command:

1 Think about the command words you would use if you were being directive. For example, 'sit down now'.
2 Add some 'fluff' words (some call them 'weasel words') – words that don't alter the meaning of the sentence you are about to utter but add a tenor of politeness. For example 'Why don't you...?' 'Why don't you sit down now?' is perfectly innocuous.
3 Mark out the command words so that they stand out a little from the rest of the sentence. Say the words 'sit down now' just a little louder than the other words. If the listener is also watching you, gesture towards their seat as you utter the words 'sit down now'.
4 Downwardly inflect the last three words so that you are using the normal commanding tonality. The effect of the downward inflection and tonal marking of the words is registered in the unconscious mind as a command, and most people will respond immediately to it.

The physical gesture makes the command even more irresistible. The example is trivial. The effect is powerful.

So the formula for creating simple embedded commands is:

● Fluff words *plus* command *using* downward inflection and tonal/physical marking

At first sight this may appear terribly contrived, but in fact you use these constructs all the time. The formula is the result of observation of how people communicate effectively, rather than a contrivance to change your ways of communicating. If you can model the effective formula purposely, then you can create powerful communications with observable results. If you feel that it is a little manipulative, then don't use it, but do be aware of how others unwittingly use the method in talking to you.

TIP *Try this little experiment in embedding commands. Invite a colleague into your office or workspace in which you have positioned two chairs. Say 'Please sit down. I don't know whether you'd like to sit here [indicating a chair and slightly upwardly inflecting the words 'sit here'] or sit down there' [indicating the other chair, downwardly inflecting the words 'sit down there' and giving those three words a little extra volume]. Your colleague will sit in the second chair.*

Anchoring emotional states and behaviours

A Russian physiologist, Ivan Pavlov, famously rang a bell each time he fed his dogs. One day he rang the bell but didn't produce the food and the dogs still salivated in anticipation. He had conditioned them to associate the sound of the bell with food. These conditioned responses are sometimes known as 'anchors' and it is possible to anchor an emotional state or behaviour in ourselves and others and then 'trigger' the same state or behaviour by repeating the original stimulus. Each one of us has thousands of these anchors already installed in us. For example, when you were a child and heard an adult using your full name and a particularly stern voice, you knew you were in trouble! When someone greets you by name and puts out their hand, you don't have to pause to consider what to do – you shake their hand and return the greeting. These are anchored responses. Let's look at how you can use anchors in practice.

Anchoring a calm state in you and others

Think of a word or phrase which captures for you the whole essence of being calm and relaxed. Now think of a physical gesture which you could make publicly without others noticing. For example, you might make a little O shape with your finger and thumb. The combination of the word/phrase and the gesture will be your anchor for a calm state.

Now find a place where you will not be disturbed, close your eyes and think back to a time when you felt completely calm, composed and relaxed. In your mind's eye, see what you saw at the time and make the image as realistic as you can – colourful, three-dimensional, vivid and detailed. Notice the physical feelings of relaxation and calm. For many of us there is a centre to those feelings, perhaps in the head or chest or stomach. Notice where the feelings are centred and allow them to spread all the way up and all the way down your body so you feel a lovely warm, peaceful sense of calm throughout your body. Now, if there are sounds associated with this time when you felt really calm and relaxed, imagine those sounds and, if it helps to imagine turning up the volume, do so. When you can see what you saw, hear what you heard, feel what you felt, anchor it by saying your word/phrase and making your gesture at exactly the same time. Now open your eyes and think of something neutral and unrelated to this calming exercise. Close your eyes again and repeat the process. You can either think of the same occasion or a different one – any time when you felt calm, relaxed and in control. Anchor it again, open your eyes and think of something neutral. Repeat the whole process four of five times and you will have anchored the calm state perfectly to your key word/phrase and gesture.

Then, any time when you want to feel calm, you simply say your key word/phrase to yourself and make your gesture and instantly you will feel a great sense of calm and wellbeing.

Imagine that you have a team member whose behaviour is erratic: sometimes they are malleable and co-operative and sometimes difficult. It's possible to anchor (effectively 'capture') their co-operative state so that you can trigger it again in future at times when they are being difficult. There's an ethical issue here, of course – you may see the use of anchors in this way as manipulative. At some level every relationship may be considered manipulative. We know what makes those close to us happy and unhappy and we often push whichever 'buttons' we need to in order to get the best out of other people. We choose our words carefully in conversation to manipulate the moods of others. Anchoring is perhaps a more focused, deliberate way of creating a particular state in someone, and you must decide whether or not you want to use the technique. Do be aware that others unwittingly anchor states in you. For example, every time someone you know utters a particular phrase or exhibits a specific behaviour, it will elicit the same response in you. That's an anchored response. The suggestion here is that you use anchors as a tool in your armoury – a way of getting someone into a particular mood so that they are easier to work with.

So, you're sitting at a table with the erratic team member. Your hand idly strays to the table top. You begin a social conversation and your team mate smiles, laughs or makes a joke. You gently and quietly tap a couple of times on the table top. The team member doesn't notice consciously, but will register unconsciously that you have done so. A minute later as the team member smiles or laughs again, tap again. You only have to do this four or five times within a few minutes and the team member will then subconsciously associate their smiling, happy mood with the taps on the table. Thereafter, each time you want the team member to return to this happy state, you simply tap on the table. Equally, you could scratch your nose, give a little cough or nod and say 'uh huh' each time you see the team member in the mood which you want to anchor. Repeating the verbal or non-verbal anchor will immediately bring them back to this state.

Calming angry people (without saying a word)

When someone is angry, they have a rush of adrenaline which is associated with the fight or flight response – if they are angry with you, the brain offers them the means to fight you or run away from you. A side-effect of undissipated adrenaline is shallow breathing. You can no more be angry whilst breathing deeply than you can sneeze with your eyes open! Intuitively, when someone is angry we might make a placatory up and down gesture with our hands, palms down and say 'calm down'. One of the worst things you can say to an angry person is 'calm down!' because it makes them even angrier. However, the hand gesture is at some level the right one – intuitively we know that if we can get someone to breathe deeper, they will stop being angry. When someone is angry they are largely focused inwards on themselves and so consciously unaware of much that is happening around them. The subconscious continues to register everything.

Imagine that you are standing and talking to an angry person. Clasp one of your forearms with the other hand. Move your thumb up and down your forearm, as though rubbing it soothingly, in time with the other person's breathing. When they are talking, they are breathing out, and every so often will need to take another breath. When they breathe in their shoulders will rise. Synchronize your thumb movements with their breathing for a number of breaths then gradually slow down your thumb movement. They will quite unconsciously begin to synchronize their breathing with your thumb movements and as their breathing slows they will become calmer. The joy of this method is that you don't need to say a word, and that's to your advantage because angry people love to throw your words back in your face. If you are sitting in view of the other person, cross your legs and allow your foot to gently move up and down in time with their breathing, gradually slowing the movement to slow their breathing and calm them down.

Now this is fine if you are face-to-face with the angry person. Sometimes you may have to calm them during a telephone call. Simply stroke a fingernail down the back of the phone in time with their talking, gradually slowing down the stroking motion and they will calm down. The secret? As you move your fingernail down the back of the phone, they will hear a faint 'Shhh, shhh' like a mother calming a small child. Because they are angry and inward focused, they won't be consciously aware of the sound, but their subconscious will register it, and they will gradually become calmer. Again, you don't have to utter a word.

Drawing out quiet people (without saying a word)

Sometimes in a meeting you'll see the quiet team member struggling to be heard. The noisy, dominant ones take over and leave no space for the quiet ones who may have something useful to say. Ask a question and extend your arms and hands as if to invite comment from the team, sweeping your hands around the room to appear to make eye contact with everyone. As you turn, ensure that the quiet person is framed inside one of your hands and make a little extra eye contact with them. Turn the other way to look around the rest of the group, hands extended, ensuring that the quiet person is framed just inside the other hand. Again, make a little extra eye contact with them. The effect is the same as if you had simply gestured with both hands toward them. They will sense that you want them to speak, have confidence in their ability to speak and are inviting them to do so.

Getting information from people reluctant to talk to you

Books on interviewing skills will tell you that, if you are dissatisfied at an answer given to one of your questions, remain silent and the other person will fill the silence out of embarrassment and give a more complete answer to your question. Unfortunately, those facing interviews have read the same books and expect that interviewers will do this. As a result, they remain silent. If you are facing someone who gives incomplete answers to your questions try this:

- Keeping your eyebrows still, lift your eyelids a little to widen your eyes. The effect is to let in more light which contracts your pupils and draws the other person's gaze.
- Tip your forehead down, just a couple of centimetres, as you continue to gaze at the other person. This is a slightly sinister look which suggests that you mean business.
- Now incline your head a couple of centimetres to one side. This effectively exposes an ear to suggest 'I'm listening'.
- Finally, tip your head back a couple of centimetres which sends out the message 'Come on – talk to me'.

The whole gesture is smooth, seamless and subtle. It's also very powerful. Typically it will get the other person to open up and tell you the things that they have been holding back. Try it on friends and family first!

The art of 'fogging' when you feel under attack

If you feel somewhat under attack from someone, it would be easy to become aggressive and fight back. Short term, this may feel good but longer term it may cause more problems than it solves. The art of verbal self-defence when under attack is to agree with the bare truth of what the other person is saying. Remember that we have to manage upwards as well as downwards in an organization. Imagine that your boss complains that your desk is always untidy. Say 'Yes, it is untidy'. Your boss has nowhere to go in the discussion now. She can't say 'Well it is untidy', because you just agreed that it was. The response to 'I see you are still driving that rubbish old car then' is 'Yes I am still driving that car'.

If someone makes a generalized statement about you, you can respond in a slightly different way. For example 'You've never been good at this, have you?' Respond with 'When did you begin to think that I was not good at this?' If they answer that you have *never* done it well, ask quietly why they had not raised the issue before. If they answer that they have noticed in the last couple of weeks/months that you have not been doing something, they will realize that they have caught themselves out with their own exaggeration and become less aggressive/assertive.

How to say 'no'

Here's another useful idea for managing upwards. Your boss presents a piece of work to you and tells you that it's urgent and must be completed by noon tomorrow. You drop everything, work madly to complete the work and present it to your boss who says either 'Oh, I hadn't expected that back so soon' or 'Leave it on the pile there and I will review it when I have the time'. Each answer suggests that the work stopped being urgent the moment it was handed to you. When someone presents you with an 'urgent' piece of work, ask 'Which part of this is urgent?' The likelihood is that nobody has ever asked that question before. After a moment's thought, the other person will probably say 'Well, I need you to make a telephone call/send an email right now'. That's fine – you can do the small urgent piece and then add the larger piece to your pile of scheduled, important but non-urgent work.

If your boss says 'This is really urgent and I need it done immediately', simply say 'Of course, and it will mean that that other urgent deadline we agreed will go back by [N] hours as a result.' Don't ask if that's OK – make it a statement. It's highly unlikely that your boss will contest it.

Another approach is a gentle reminder of the other deadlines you have agreed with your boss and then a polite request to help you to prioritize.

A final approach is to say that you have no spare capacity to do this other piece of work right now, but you will find someone in your team to do it. If your boss insists that you do it, use one of the other techniques in response.

Summary

Positive language implants in people's minds the image of the things we want them to focus on and we should strive to avoid negative language in influencing others. Replacing the word 'but' with the word 'and' conveys a more positive message and can even make contradictions seem acceptable to others. If you are arguing a particular case, the word 'because' is a powerful justification in its own right. An embedded command works at the subconscious level, helping the listener to accept something of which they may not consciously be aware. Through anchoring we can bring people back to a particular emotional state or preferred behaviour and we can also anchor a calm state in ourselves, which may help us to deal more effectively with difficult people. Through gesture alone, we can calm angry people, draw out quiet people and get information from someone reluctant to talk to us. 'Fogging' helps us to stave off verbal attacks from others. Finally, develop the art of saying 'no' without saying 'no' directly and notice how much easier your life becomes as a result!

SUNDAY

MONDAY

TUESDAY

WEDNESDAY

THURSDAY

FRIDAY

SATURDAY

Fact-check (answers at the back)

1 The true meaning of a communication is:
a) Obvious from your intentions ❏
b) The response which it elicits ❏
c) Immaterial ❏
d) The response which you expected ❏

2 When someone asks you to do a piece of work urgently, you should say:
a) 'Give it to someone else to do' ❏
b) 'I haven't got the time to do that now' ❏
c) 'Which part of this is urgent?' ❏
d) 'Why do you always pick on me? ❏

3 The art of 'fogging' is:
a) Agreeing with the bare truth of a criticism ❏
b) Being vague in your answer to a criticism ❏
c) Disagreeing with a criticism ❏
d) Ignoring the person who criticizes you ❏

4 One way to draw out a quiet person is:
a) Telling them to speak up, because nobody can hear them ❏
b) To take them to one side and tell them that you expect them to contribute more in future ❏
c) To ignore them to the point at which they feel obliged to speak up ❏
d) Gesturally, by 'framing' them with your hands ❏

5 The formula for creating embedded commands is:
a) Fluff words *plus* command *using* downward inflection and tonal/physical marking ❏
b) Fluff words *plus* command *using* upward inflection and tonal/physical marking ❏
c) Fluff words *plus* command *using* neutral inflection and tonal/physical marking ❏
d) Fluff words *plus* command *using* downward inflection and no tonal/physical marking ❏

6 The effect of the word 'but' is to:
a) Strengthen your argument ❏
b) Erase everything which preceded it ❏
c) Make your meaning clearer ❏
d) Show the other person that you are correct ❏

7 One of the reasons why small children misbehave is because:
a) They don't know any better ❏
b) They don't listen to what we tell them ❏
c) We tell them what to do and they ignore us ❏
d) We tell them what not to do ❏

8 'Because' can strengthen an argument:
a) When the stakes are relatively high ❏
b) When neither side has anything to gain ❏
c) When the stakes are relatively low ❏
d) When the matter is urgent ❏

9 To get information from someone reluctant to talk:
a) Narrow your eyes, tip your head sideways, downwards and back ❏
b) Widen your eyes, tip your head backwards, sideways and down ❏
c) Narrow your eyes, tip your head forward, sideways and back ❏
d) Widen your eyes, tip your head forward, sideways and back ❏

10 Anchoring:
a) Conditions us to associate a stimulus with a response ❏
b) Deflects us from what's actually happening through confusion ❏
c) Conditions us to believe that the other person is right ❏
d) Helps us to punish our staff for wrong-doing ❏

WEDNESDAY

Managing specific types of difficult behaviour

Today we are going to look at the commonest types of difficult behaviour and some ways of managing them. This chapter can be used as a reference guide, showing the chief characteristics of each type and a method of managing them. In many of the cases you'll encounter here, direct feedback is an option. On Thursday we'll look at delivering feedback that really works and at setting task and behavioural objectives. In this chapter we focus primarily on how we can encourage changes in the behaviour of difficult people at work without giving that direct feedback.

Some of the types we'll meet here are insecure, some are attention-seekers, some are downright aggressive and some seem to have lost any spark of joy in life. In a long working career you'll meet them all, and the better you are armed to deal with them, the less disruptive they will be to you and your team. Generally, you don't need to be too harsh with these people – a well-considered, gentle approach is often enough to wake them up to the effects of their behaviour. Most of them don't do what they do with any sense of malice and are often oblivious to the effect they have on others. Sometimes you need to hold up the mirror to them and show them those effects; sometimes you simply need to steer them back towards more productive work.

ASSERTIVE

AGGRESSIVE   PASSIVE

In each case, look at the underlying reasons for the behaviour. Behaviour serves a purpose and we may or may not be consciously aware of that purpose. In managing difficult people try to see the world from their point of view and rather than fighting against them, work with their subjective view to change their thinking.

Type	Characteristics	How to manage them
Abuser of privileges	Takes things too far and takes advantage of others' good will	It's likely that they behave this way because nobody has challenged it before and they know that they can get away with it. Their behaviour is rarely based on malicious intent, and more on having fun and enjoying what they can whilst it appears to be available. You need to be firm, and re-establish the boundaries within which you expect them to work. Indicate clearly where they have overstepped the mark and ask them to consider in future that teams work well when the members can trust each other to behave fairly towards each other.

Aggressor	Highly aggressive	Aggressive behaviour, paradoxically, is often based in deep insecurity – a fear of losing control and an overcompensation to establish that control. Often, too, aggressive people lack self-awareness and as long as nobody challenges them, they continue to behave in this way because it gets them results. Let them say what they have to say without immediately reacting to them. Always address them by name to establish control. Then clearly state the boundaries within which you and they will work. Never be drawn into a public argument with them. The louder they are, the quieter you should speak to them.
Alien	Appears to be on another planet	The person who marches to the beat of a different drum doesn't necessarily do so to be different but has, over years, developed a persona which seems out of step with everyone else's. It's not our job to change that persona – it's our job in managing them to ensure that they work as well as possible. Don't try to get them to conform to a work-based stereotype. If this person is genuinely a good worker, let them be themselves, show you value their contribution and do what you can to nurture their talents. Avoid placing them in a leadership position because others will not readily follow them and help them to specialize in their own unique area. If they are not good workers, then that's a different issue which can be addressed through closer management, good objective setting and monitoring and realistic appraisal of capability. Try if you can to separate the character of the person from the quality of their work.

Type	Characteristics	How to manage them
Baby	'It's not fair.' Negative view of everything	The baby is an attention seeker, so give them some of the attention they want – show that you are really listening to what they say. Do not agree with their negative statements and when you answer them, speak factually, giving the positive side of each idea and addressing the whole team and not just them. Reinforce the positives at work, realistically rather than in any forced way and offer simple, rational statements when they display negativity. Ensure that you are scrupulously fair so that they have no factual basis on which to level accusations of unfairness. If they complain that someone has better work than them, ask them what they would like to do and, if possible, give them more stretching work to focus their minds on something constructive. If they have requested more interesting work they forfeit the right to complain about it.
Class clown	Turns everything into a joke	The class clown seems unable to be serious about anything. If they are disruptive to others or if their work is suffering as a result of their attitude, you need to give them that direct feedback. If they are simply annoying you, be selective about what you laugh at. Smile after a joke and immediately turn the conversation to work, asking, for example, about their progress on a piece of work with a gentle reminder of your expectations. If there is a social committee, persuade them to join it.
Complainer	Nothing is ever quite as they want it	Often people complain about things over which they have little or no control. It's easier to be negative about something from the outside than the inside. Give them duties which force them to think about the way things are done in the team. For example, rotate the chairmanship of team meetings and give them the first opportunity to take the chair; ask them

		to review some long-standing procedures or processes and document viable alternatives. Effectively, you are giving them the chance to lead in areas where they would normally complain. As they begin to work in those areas they forfeit the right to complain about them.
Controller	Needs to shape the world their own way	Like the aggressor, the controller feels unhappy unless they can be in control. Don't argue or listen to this person's opinions, but calmly express your opinions, and don't be intimidated. Demonstrate strength without argument, and give them room and time to respond. If possible, give them a specific duty which is unique to them and tell the rest of the group that they have this responsibility. The new found status will be important to them and they will relish having a work area which is theirs to control. Give them some freedom to organize this area in their own way and praise them when they do it well.
Gossip	Tells stories about other people	Gossips live vicariously, often finding their own lives so lacking in excitement that they focus on others. They are often blissfully unaware of the effects of their gossiping. Let them know each time they begin to gossip that you have no interest in their stories. Alternatively, ask them for very specific details of the incidents which they are describing and when, inevitably, they are unable to answer, suggest to them that it is very dangerous to tell tales when you don't have all the facts at your disposal. Tell them directly that if they are prepared to gossip about others, their own team mates will not trust them and they should be careful not to isolate themselves from the others. At a team meeting raise the issue of gossip and destructive talk, without accusing the individual. Ask the team how they feel about it and perhaps the team gossip will get the message from the others that it is unacceptable.

Type	Characteristics	How to manage them
Incessant talker	Never stops talking	Don't be shy to interrupt them. Use your interruptions to guide them back to work – 'It's nice to talk but this isn't getting the work done.' Segue into a new, work-related topic. Be very direct with them, using their name to get their attention. Give them a time check, telling them that you only have another 30 seconds before each of you needs to continue with your work. Indicate to them that others in the group need periods of quiet to focus on their work and ask them to be sensitive to that. Try joking that you can't get a word in edgewise. If all else fails, give them direct feedback (see Thursday).
Indecisive	Can't make a decision and spends an inordinate amount of time gathering facts to defer decision-making	For the indecisive person, the world is fraught with difficulties. Their fear of failure constantly stops them taking action. Acknowledge that they have concerns and allow them to voice them. Do it one-to-one and not publicly. Gain agreement in stages, rather than pushing for big decisions and then set them clear objectives and ensure their understanding so they can commit to positive action. In this way slowly ease them into making more complex decisions and building their confidence in their ability to make the right decision.
Know-all and Claim-to-know-it-all	Expert in everything	The know-all genuinely knows a lot and is keen that everyone else should be aware of their encyclopaedic knowledge; the claim-to-know-it-all has an opinion which may or may not be based in fact and will express it regardless. Ask the former to demonstrate how their facts relate to the current work situation and show that, while you value the facts, you value their practical application at work even more. For the latter, present your facts and ideas as alternatives which they may want to consider, rather than absolute facts and in both cases ensure that they are aware that other people need space to give their own opinions and demonstrate their own knowledge.

Lazybones	Too lazy to focus on work; under-achiever	Set them realistic but stretching objectives, ensuring that you meet regularly for progress reports. Don't ever appear to agree with them when they (as they inevitably will) offer excuses for their lack of achievement. Indicate that others in the team (unnamed) are achieving a great deal in the same working circumstances and make it clear to them that they are falling behind the standards you expect of them. Use the CASE structure (see Thursday) to set them a behavioural objective, to show that you really mean business.
Low contributor	Contributes little or nothing to the team	Ask them an open-ended question in a meeting and wait (even if it seems as if you are waiting for an eternity) until they break the silence. Ask them privately if there is something troubling them and again wait patiently for a reply.
'Mood hoover'	Sucks the positive energy out of a group through negative outlook	Give them very direct feedback (see Thursday) on the effects that they are having on their colleagues, and reflect, realistically, the very positive things that are happening within the group. If the mood hoover is ambitious, make it abundantly clear that people follow those who inspire them positively and that negativity is an undesirable trait in leadership and will halt their progress at work.
NIICHI (not if I can help it)	Strongly resists change	Don't give them a platform to influence the rest of the group. Enlist them during periods of change as a 'reality checker', showing that you respect their views which you know are based on experience of what has and has not worked before, so that they can help you to shape change that works. Often the NIICHI is scared of change because it makes them feel out of control. Given a central role in shaping the change gives them back their sense of control and they can be turned round to think a great deal more positively if they see that you take them seriously rather than fighting against them.

Type	Characteristics	How to manage them
No confidence	Doesn't have any sense of their own ability and fights shy of responsibility	Paradoxically, the person who lacks confidence is often more fearful of success than of failure. With success comes responsibility and accountability – do something well once and all eyes are on you to do it again. So efforts to convince the person with no confidence of their ability may be misguided because their ability isn't the real issue. Give them some small responsibility which they can exercise out of the public eye and gradually build on that responsibility so their confidence in success builds. Too much too soon can be damaging so be patient as you allow them to build on their successes, understanding that it's OK to take responsibility and that, far from adding pressure, it can make work more stimulating and enjoyable and help them become more popular within the group.
Passive-aggressive	Criticizes indirectly through sniping and sarcasm. Never confronts an issue directly	Passive-aggressive people are snipers, taking pot-shots from the shadows. There is an element of cowardice in their approach and they need to learn that, if they want to be successful, they must tackle real issues head on and refrain from remarking on things which are not important. They need to learn, too, that their behaviour will isolate them from others who will not trust them with sensitive information.Keep refocusing them on the issues rather than people. It will take time, but they will ultimately realize that you will not take the bait. Instruct those working closely with them to do the same. If they cannot get the reaction they want from you and the team they will stop trying. Tell them directly that they are in danger of making themselves unpopular with others and, if they are ambitious, make it clear that this behaviour is not acceptable at any level and will certainly hamper their progress to more senior positions.

Procrastinator	Never does today what could be done tomorrow	Often, procrastinators learnt very early in their life that they could leave something to the last minute and still succeed with the pressure brought by a touch deadline. They do tend to work well under pressure. The issue here is not so much when they do their work but the standard of their work if they leave it late to begin. If they do miss deadlines, set reasonable, but stretching, objectives with regular reporting at set milestones. Help them plan their work to meet deadlines and make it clear that you expect work to be delivered on time.
Rude	Rude and sarcastic to others; insensitive to others' feelings	Use the EEC formula (see Thursday) to give them feedback on the effect of their behaviour on others.
Smelly	Has personal hygiene problems	This is a tricky one and unfortunately quite common. You simply have to tackle it head on. Tell them privately that you and others have noticed that they have an odour issue and explain that this can make it uncomfortable for others working in close proximity to them. I once had this conversation with someone who said that he had allergic reactions to soap. He was unaware of the existence of hypoallergenic soap. He tried it and his problem disappeared. You have to take the bit between your teeth here and remember that this is as embarrassing for the malodorous person as it is for you.
Sycophant	They will agree with everything you say and it's difficult to tell what they actually think for themselves	Help them to avoid conflict situations and to feel secure. Show a real interest in their opinions on things which are not critical to work or are non-controversial. Then ease into work-related conversations and ask for their opinion before proffering your own. Encourage them to think for themselves. Ask them to consider a piece of work and come back to you with their view on how they should tackle it before discussing the detail with them.

Type	Characteristics	How to manage them
Victim	The world is against them, and they will find all the evidence to prove it	Do not allow them to speak on behalf of others and challenge them when they attempt to do so. Challenge their generalized, exaggerated statements and calmly ask for evidence of their assertions. Give them feedback (see Thursday) on the effect that they are having on those around them.
Yes but, no but	Says 'yes' then doesn't deliver (aka the 'crowd pleaser')	Reduce the number of mission-critical pieces of work given to this person; work with them to establish their outstanding tasks and help them to prioritize; check their progress regularly and gently caution them when they allow themselves to be distracted. Insist, having delegated some work, that they take on no other work until yours is finished.

Summary

Difficult behaviour manifests itself in many forms and no single solution works in every case. When you encounter a difficult person ask yourself what they might gain from their behaviour. All our behaviour serves some purpose, whether or not we are consciously aware of it and if you can determine or subtly unearth the underlying purpose, you are far better placed to deal with it.

Difficult as it may be, set your judgements to one side and be careful, too, to deal with the issue and not the person. If you show disdain for the person exhibiting difficult behaviour they are likely to dig their heels in and continue to behave the same way to spite you. See the world from their point of view and work from that viewpoint to find ways of changing their mind.

Don't challenge behaviour simply because it doesn't match your own, but manage behaviours which cause problems in the workplace for you, for others and also for the person displaying the behaviour who may unwittingly be halting their own progression through the organization. Show empathy where necessary, be calm and be rational.

SUNDAY
MONDAY
TUESDAY
WEDNESDAY
THURSDAY
FRIDAY
SATURDAY

Fact-check (answers at the back)

1 In dealing with an aggressive person:
a) As they raise their voice, ensure that you raise yours in equal measure ❑
b) Shout at them from the outset to show who is boss ❑
c) The louder they talk, the quieter you should talk ❑
d) The louder they talk, the more silent you should become ❑

2 When someone constantly complains:
a) Give them the chance to change the areas about which they complain ❑
b) Tell them to get on with their work and stop complaining ❑
c) Tell them you agree with everything they say ❑
d) Tell them to stop being ridiculous ❑

3 In dealing with the incessant talker:
a) Never interrupt them ❑
b) Use an interruption to guide them back to work ❑
c) Just let them talk – at least they liven up the workplace ❑
d) Tell them to be quiet because they are annoying you and everyone else ❑

4 When dealing with an indecisive person:
a) Give them a really big, mission-critical decision to help them practise ❑
b) Never give them any decisions to make, because they are incapable of making them ❑
c) Push them really hard over every decision ❑
d) Gain agreement in stages, to ease them towards decision-making ❑

5 If you are managing a lazy person:
a) Accept readily their reasons for non-delivery of work ❑
b) Set them stretching objectives and meet them regularly to assess their progress ❑
c) Tell them that they are the laziest person you have ever met ❑
d) Don't worry about it – you can always delegate work to more willing people ❑

6 When someone contributes very little to the team:
a) Ask them a question publicly and demand an instant response ❑
b) Never question them publicly because it might embarrass them ❑
c) Ask them a question publicly and wait as long as necessary for their reply ❑
d) Accept that they don't want to contribute and spend your time with people who do ❑

7 In managing a passive-aggressive person:

a) Shout at them, telling them their behaviour is unacceptable ❏

b) Fight sarcasm with sarcasm – it's the only thing they will understand ❏

c) Refocus them on the issues and not the people ❏

d) Ask your team to give them the silent treatment ❏

8 If someone is always putting work off until 'later':

a) Give them unachievable deadlines to test them ❏

b) Extend their deadlines to give them longer to finish their work ❏

c) Don't worry about it – we all miss deadlines sometimes ❏

d) Help them plan and prioritize their work ❏

9 If someone is constantly sycophantic:

a) Revel in it – it's nice that they are trying so hard to please you ❏

b) Let them formulate their own approach to a piece of work before discussing it with them ❏

c) Show favouritism towards them, because you know they work hard to please you ❏

d) Show them up in front of the whole team ❏

10 When someone acts as a victim:

a) Sympathize with them, because they are probably having a hard time ❏

b) Berate the team for bullying them ❏

c) Apologize for making them feel that way ❏

d) Challenge them when they say they are speaking on behalf of others ❏

THURSDAY

Feedback that works and critical conversations

One of the key skills for a good manager is the ability to give critical and constructive feedback. It is perhaps the area which causes the greatest anxiety, too. Very often a manager will be more anxious about delivering feedback than the recipient is in hearing it. Often, too, the recipient will accept feedback without challenge, knowing that their behaviour was out of line and even surprised that it took so long for you to address it.

It's vital that you give feedback as early as you can. If you tackle someone about a behaviour which they have displayed for months or years, they have every right to ask you why you didn't address it much sooner. Early feedback prevents later escalation. Be careful not to jump in too early. If someone is generally very easy to work with and displays one single instance of errant behaviour then it may well be a glitch, caused by a specific incident. In every aspect of management you need to strike a balance, and in managing difficult behaviour you will often be dealing with apparent growing trends and differences in behaviour.

Today, we suggest that good feedback is neither 'positive' nor 'negative' but a 'gift of information', offer two models for structuring effective feedback that sticks, and explore ways of managing critical conversations with difficult team members. Most organizations have established systems for creating task- or output-based objectives, often using the SMART mnemonic to ensure completeness. Equally useful, but less common, are behavioural objectives, which can be set using the CASE structure.

General principles of giving feedback

- Remain calm
- Focus on the single issue at the centre of the feedback
- Make the feedback the only topic of the conversation, avoiding 'fluff' and social talk
- Focus on behaviours which can be changed; avoid discussion of personality
- Use 'I' when you describe your experience of the other person's behaviour
- Avoid bringing other names into the feedback – make it a two-way conversation
- Always give specific examples
- If describing unacceptable behaviour, make it clear why the behaviour is unacceptable – the effect it is having
- Feedback is not about you, and you need to be sensitive to the recipient. Equally, they must be left in no doubt about the message of the feedback
- Be congruent – your voice, words and body language should all be giving the same message
- Give the recipient time to think, reflect and answer
- Listen when the recipient is talking
- Avoid overload – it is better to tackle a single issue in a single session
- Work towards a positive outcome and actions

Give the person time to change their behaviour. For some it will be instant and for others it may take time. If you have to invoke disciplinary proceedings against someone, one of the measures of your fair and reasonable treatment of the person will be that you gave them sufficient time to amend their behaviour.

Old and new ways of delivering feedback – the staleness of the 'positive sandwich'

Early in my corporate life I was taught how to give feedback, using what was known then as the *positive sandwich*. Over time, its name transmuted into something a little more vulgar. It was the standard way to offer feedback to someone displaying inappropriate behaviour. The idea was that, rather than approach the topic head on, we should offer a positive statement (the lower slice of bread), slip in the feedback about the behavioural issue (the filling) and finally offer another positive statement (the top slice of bread) to send our team-mate away, presumably still feeling loved. The problem was that the positive statements diluted the statement in the middle. The team member was left not really understanding the issue and certainly not the importance of rectifying the aberrant behaviour. It became a joke with us. 'Hi Fred – that's a really nice shirt you're wearing. Your work's rubbish, but your shirt's really nice.' What's the message here?

THAT'S A LOVELY TIE, BUT...

Managers often apologize for giving feedback. 'Erm, Fred – I didn't want to have to raise this with you, but, well the thing is...' Ensure that when you do give feedback, that's the whole conversation, with no niceties or fluffy stuff on either side of the feedback. That way, the feedback is more powerful.

Feedback is a gift of information. The recipient of a gift can choose to use it now and cherish it, store it for later use, ignore it or pass it on to someone else. Push to one side the notion of positive and negative feedback – that's largely irrelevant. Our aim in giving feedback is either to enhance performance or to change behaviour. The key is that the recipient should understand the effects of particular behaviour. Very often, people do things inappropriately at work because they have not understood the effects of what they do, and sometimes have not understood that their actions cause any effects at all.

Well-structured feedback should either encourage someone to continue to do something appropriate or stop doing something inappropriate. Either way, the recipient should understand the effects of their actions.

A feedback formula – EEC

Here's a simple and elegant structure for delivering feedback (EEC):

- **E**xample – a specific example or examples of the behaviour you have witnessed
- **E**ffects – the effects of the behaviour on you or others
- **C**ontinue/**C**hange – if it was good, do it again; if it wasn't what will you do instead?

(**E**xample) Pat, on Tuesday when the new person, Julia, joined the department and I was away for the day, she said that you

---

took her under your wing, introduced her to everyone in the group, showed her around and generally made her feel really welcome. (**E**ffects) She said you had made her feel very welcome and she was absolutely delighted. (**C**ontinue) Thank you very much for doing this – I really appreciate it. When our new joiner, Fred, starts tomorrow, would you mind showing him round, as you did Julia?

Here we're using the formula to recognize good behaviour. It's clean and elegant and motivating. Now let's imagine that Pat had ignored Julia...

> (**E**xample) Pat, on Tuesday when the new person, Julia, joined the department and I was away for the day, I understand that she was left alone for pretty much the whole day. Neither you nor anyone else introduced yourselves to her and she was left to find her own way round. (**E**ffects) She was really put out and felt terribly unwelcome in the group. (**C**hange) We have another new joiner, Fred, starting tomorrow. What can you do to make him feel more welcome than Julia?

Notice that in the case of the inappropriate behaviour, we ask the recipient of the feedback to tell us what they will do differently. This is important – if we instruct them they don't 'own' the issue in the same way as if they determine the change in their own behaviour. The act of saying what they will do forms more of a verbal contract than simply nodding assent to suggestions that we make for them and tends to result more often in changed behaviour.

The EEC formula is great for giving instant feedback on straightforward issues. A different formula, EENC, is particularly useful for more serious issues.

Giving feedback on more serious issues – EENC

- **E**xample – what they did **E**motions – how you feel (described but not demonstrated)
- **N**eeds – what they need to do differently
- **C**onsequences – what will happen if they do or don't change their behaviour

Let's look at an example. Here, we'll show some feedback delivered as a monologue to illustrate the structure. In reality, it should be a two-way conversation and we'll look in a moment at how that works.

(**E**xample) Pat – I notice that you have not attended the last three team meetings, when you know that they are our main way of monitoring progress against team objectives and sharing information across the team. (**E**motions) I'm disappointed that you have neither attended the team meetings, nor informed me that you would not be attending. (**N**eeds) I need to see you not only attend the next three team meetings, but to contribute as actively as the other team members. (**C**onsequences) If you do, I am prepared to treat your recent absences as an oversight. If you don't, you know that I will have to take this to a more formal level.

Pat is left in no doubt about the seriousness of the issue and the consequences and is unlikely to miss the next meeting.

Let's unravel this a little. When you are giving behavioural feedback you should be talking about an observed *change* in behaviour. After all, if you were to challenge Pat for not attending a meeting in the last five years, Pat has every right to ask why you have waited five years before giving any feedback.

In using EENC as the structure for a dialogue with Pat, you might say: 'Pat – you always used to attend our team meetings, which you know are our main way of monitoring progress against team objectives and sharing information across the group. I notice that you have not attended the last three team meetings. What's changed?' Now Pat may have a viable reason for non-attendance, although you should also have been informed. Asking 'what's changed?' gives Pat a fair chance to explain.

It's important that you describe your feeling about Pat's behaviour without displaying it. Shrieking 'You make me so mad!' is counter-productive. Remain calm and you demonstrate self-control. Become angry and the loss of control sends a message to Pat that it's OK to be like this. Remember that everything that you do and say as a manager gives your team members permission to do and say the same things, so it's important to maintain dignity and self-control. The word 'disappointed' is a great one to use here. It's the kind of word a parent or teacher would use in addressing a naughty child and it's painful to hear as an adult.

Rather than telling Pat the behaviours you want to see, ask Pat what he should do differently. He will tell you that he should attend the meetings in future, and you can prompt him to suggest that he should contribute, too.

Finally, either you can suggest the possible consequences to Pat, or turn things round and say 'Look, if we reversed roles and I had not come along to the meetings, nor told you that I wasn't coming, what would you do?' Pat will tend to design a harsher punishment for himself than you would have suggested, so here you can appear a little lenient and suggest treating the behaviour as an oversight, while saying that you will take it to a more formal level if it happens again. Pat will be at once relieved and yet keen to avoid a repeat of this conversation.

The EENC technique is powerful and the recipient of the feedback rarely reoffends.

After delivering any feedback, record it. One of the commonest causes of failure in disciplinary hearings is the lack of documented evidence produced by the manager. If you delivered feedback using EEC, document it – send an email confirming what you said. If you have delivered feedback using EENC, not only document it, but ask the recipient of the email to write an acknowledgement that the email is a fair record of the conversation. This audit trail may be very important if the individual continues to behave inappropriately.

TIP

Remember that when giving feedback you should always be talking about changes in behaviour rather than long-standing issues which were previously unaddressed. If you leave it too long to raise an issue you effectively forfeit the right to raise it and the difficult person has every right to ask why you didn't question it before now if you have seen it as an issue for a long time. This highlights the need to deal with growing trends or patterns of difficult behaviour as early as possible to prevent their escalation.

Creating behavioural objectives

You may be familiar with the mnemonic SMART, widely used for creating task-based objectives. It's not a useful formula for documenting behavioural objectives because it focuses on what's measurable, and it isn't always possible to measure behavioural change. It is, however, possible to monitor and observe it.

An alternative – CASE – is designed specifically to address behavioural issues:

- **C**ontext – what behaviour have you witnessed and in what context?
- **A**ction(s) – what action should the individual take to address the issue?
- **S**tandards – what are the organization's standards which the individual has failed to uphold?
- **E**valuation – how will you monitor, give feedback and evaluate the changes in the individual's behaviour?

You have a choice in the way you write CASE objectives. You can either write them in the third person ('X did this and then she did that') or in the first person ('I did this and I did that'). There is real power in getting the individual to agree to an objective in the first person. It becomes an informal contract (and perhaps a type of confession, too!)

I generally ask the individual to date and sign the objective and I will date and sign it too, reinforcing the notion that it forms a contract between you. It's also useful to have signed and dated evidence, should the behaviour escalate and become subject to more formal disciplinary proceedings. Here's an example, written for someone who has been using the internet for personal reasons during working hours. In this case it's written in the third person.

Context: On six occasions in the last two weeks, Judy has been using the internet for her own purposes during working hours, evidenced by the usage log supplied by the IT department

Action: Judy will refrain from using the internet for any private purposes during core working hours

---

Standards: This is in accordance with Section 4, Clause 6 of the staff handbook which states: 'Any employee may access the internet for private purposes outside core working hours, providing they do so within the standards set out in Appendix 4.'

Evaluation: I (David Cotton) will monitor the IT log fortnightly for the next two months to ensure that Judy does not use the internet for personal reasons, after which I will monitor her usage once monthly for the following three months.

Date: Signed (David Cotton)........Signed (Judy Harrison).............

The CASE objective may look a little harsh, but in practice it is often enough to ensure that a behavioural issue doesn't escalate to a more formal level. Disciplinary proceedings can be difficult and stressful. The CASE objective may be enough to nip in the bud something which would continue and grow if left unchecked.

Summary

If you can give feedback effectively, you are well on the way to managing difficult people. Ensuring that your feedback is structured, using the EEC or EENC formula, will give you comfort that you are getting it right, increase your credibility and, most importantly, give a clear message to the recipient that their behaviour has been noticed, is not acceptable and must change. Giving early feedback will reduce the likelihood of repeated bad behaviour and help you to avoid a more awkward discussion later.

However you choose to give feedback, offer it calmly and rationally, with good and incontrovertible examples. Describe the effects of the behaviour on work standards, you, other people, productivity or whatever is relevant to that behaviour and always work towards a positive outcome or action. Avoid apologizing because giving feedback is part of your role, and set aside thoughts of positive and negative feedback in favour of feedback as information.

SUNDAY
MONDAY
TUESDAY
WEDNESDAY
THURSDAY
FRIDAY
SATURDAY

For relatively small issues, use the EEC formula and for major issues, the EENC structure. Document your discussions afterwards so that, should things be taken to a more formal level, you have an audit trail.

Create behavioural objectives using the CASE structure and, if your organization allows it, get the recipient to sign and date it as an agreed statement of the objective.

Fact-check (answers at the back)

1 The positive sandwich:
a) Is a good way to give feedback, because it makes the recipient feel better ❑
b) Is a poor way to give feedback, because it dilutes the real message ❑
c) Is the best feedback method, because the recipient hears two pieces of good news to one bad ❑
d) Is effective in delivering bad news ❑

2 Managers should:
a) Always apologize before giving feedback ❑
b) Deliver feedback and demand an apology from the team member ❑
c) Deliver feedback in an accusing way to leave the team member in no doubt about what they have done ❑
d) Never apologize before giving feedback ❑

3 Well-structured feedback should:
a) Encourage the team member either to continue or to stop doing something ❑
b) Make the recipient feel very guilty ❑
c) Make the recipient feel very small ❑
d) Be designed to show the team what a good manager you are ❑

4 The EEC formula is designed:
a) To give instant feedback on serious and complex issues ❑
b) To give a warning before a disciplinary issue ❑
c) To give instant feedback on straightforward issues ❑
d) To give instant feedback on something absolutely trivial ❑

5 EENC stands for:
a) Example, Evidence, Needs, Consequences ❑
b) Evidence, Emotions, Needs, Consequences ❑
c) Evidence, Effect, Needs, Consequences ❑
d) Example, Emotions, Needs, Consequences ❑

6 CASE is used for:
a) Task-based objectives ❑
b) Attitudinal objectives ❑
c) Behavioural objectives ❑
d) Social objectives ❑

7 In giving feedback:
a) It is not necessary to give specific examples when talking about behaviours ❑
b) It is best to deliver feedback as a monologue rather than as a two-way process ❑
c) It is best to tackle every outstanding issue to clear the air ❑
d) It is best to restrict the number of issues (ideally to one) that you tackle in one session ❑

8 In giving feedback:
a) It is the words which count ❑
b) It is the body language which gives the true message ❑
c) It is important that the words, voice and body language give the same message ❑
d) It is not important how you deliver the message as long as the other person gets the point ❑

9 In giving feedback:
a) It's important to give specific examples ❑
b) It's not important to give specific examples ❑
c) It's fine to talk about general trends of behaviour without being specific ❑
d) It's fine to tell the person that the whole group agrees with your viewpoint ❑

10 In giving feedback:
a) Embed it in a social conversation to take the sting out of it ❑
b) Make it the sole topic of the conversation ❑
c) Introduce it by stealth into a different conversation ❑
d) Ensure that the conversation is as wide-ranging as possible, incidentally including your feedback ❑

FRIDAY

Managing conflict

Conflict is a necessary and inevitable aspect of working life. People have different beliefs, values and perceptions, and conflicting attitudes can cover underlying tensions. Well managed, a certain level of conflict can be useful, stimulating creativity and motivating through healthy competition.

When the conflict becomes too serious, it can be terribly damaging to morale, team spirit and productivity. Today we look at how conflict may arise and how to manage it. We also explore cultural differences in what may be perceived to be conflict and what may be seen as relatively normal working interaction. We all come to work with certain needs and desires and if these are not met, then conflict may result. It can be internal – a personal struggle or difficulty, or external – when it flares up between two or more people.

How conflict arises

The reasons why conflict arises are many and varied, and it's important to be alert to the underlying causes. Simply handling conflict on a case by case basis without looking to see whether there are underlying trends which caused the conflict may be a recipe for long-term disaster. Some of the commonest causes of conflict are listed below, along with possible preventative solutions:

Causes of conflict	Possible solutions
Poor communication	Examine your own communication style. Are you as open and transparent as possible? Do you disseminate information fairly and evenly? Are you approachable?
Weak leadership	If this refers to someone above you in the hierarchy, there may be little you can do directly, but you can ensure that you display strong leadership within your own area
Personal grudges and grievances	Management by wandering around will expose you to the cliques, the alliances, and the people at odds with each other. Be observant and deal with niggling personal issues before they escalate. Be aware, too, of office politics and be sensitive to genuine grievances which may not have been addressed or have been addressed unsatisfactorily for the individuals involved
Envy of someone else's work or role	Be even-handed in delegation of work, showing no favouritism (even if you feel it)
Lack of recognition for achievement	Ensure that you give praise when it is due. Don't gush, but be careful to give appropriate levels of recognition for jobs well done, additional effort and particular achievements
A sense of unfairness or lack of transparency	Take time every now and then to reflect on how you distribute work, information and praise, who you have rated highly in appraisals and why and check that you are maintaining transparency and fairness in all your actions. If your own bosses are not acting fairly, have the courage to challenge them and point out the effects on your team, their morale and productivity
Fear (of change, of other people, of job loss)	If you are truly approachable and open in your communication you should see little of this. It's interesting that leaders only talk about winning hearts and minds in times of change and yet, if they inspired people to think they were worthy leaders in times of stability, change would be a great deal easier and the fear factor less important.

Boredom	Give people work which stretches them. Rather than delegate to someone you know can do a piece of work, if time permits, give it to someone for whom it is new and challenging with plenty of guidance and support to set them up for success. Rotate duties, roles and responsibilities so that everyone has a chance to experience more variety in their work

How to defuse tense situations

When there is conflict between two or more individuals, separate them and ask them to describe as objectively and dispassionately as possible how they see the issue. Only when they have explained separately and you have ascertained the facts should you bring them together to work through the issue.

Set clear ground rules, e.g.:

- No raised voices
- No personal attacks
- Just the facts
- A genuine attempt to resolve the problem rather than rake over old fires

Show each party respect, by listening to them and insisting that they listen to each other and give each other space to air their grievances. Be firm in stating the solution and clear that you will continue to monitor the situation and talk to each of them. Document your discussions (one of the reasons that disciplinary hearings fail is because of lack of documented evidence that anything took place before the hearing).

Managing bullies and bullying at work

Bullying is widespread and not always easy to detect. If someone at work is accused of bullying, take the allegation seriously and be very careful to investigate thoroughly before tackling the alleged bully. Talk to your HR department about the allegations and ask for their support – it's important that you deal with it according to your organizational policies and that you do so as quickly as possible so that it doesn't escalate.

There are four major types of bullying:

- Undermining professional status (e.g. questioning competence, public humiliation)
- Undermining a person (e.g. belittling, delegating meaningless tasks, teasing and name calling)
- Isolating a person (e.g. excluding them from conversations, withholding information)
- Overworking someone (e.g. giving them unachievable deadlines, putting undue pressure on them)

When you become aware that someone may be bullying others:

- Separate the bully from the bullied
- Ask the person making the allegation to:
  - note each incident in detail
  - try and remain calm and not show overt emotion towards the alleged bully – this is simply playing into their hands

Observe the alleged bully closely to see if you detect any signs of bullying. If you don't, it doesn't mean that it isn't happening; bullies can be highly manipulative and subtle in their approaches. Note, too, that just because someone accuses someone else of bullying that doesn't mean it *is* happening; it may be that the accuser has a 'victim' mentality or the chemistry is simply wrong between the accuser and accused. Either way, you have to take it seriously and it's best to involve HR rather than tackle it alone.

De-escalating power games

There are two types of power – external (the power we attribute to people because of their position, knowledge, etc.) and internal (the power that we appear to exude from the inside out).

Let's look at some types of external power:

- **Legitimate** The power that comes from being in a position of recognized authority
- **Reward** The power that comes from being in a position of being able to give or withhold something that someone else wants

- **Coercive** The power that comes from being able to threaten unpleasant consequences if someone else does not conform to your requirements
- **Expert** The power that comes from having subject expertise
- **Connection** The power that comes from knowing the right people in the right positions
- **Information** The power that comes from being perceived to have information which others do not have
- **Negative** The power that comes from being able to stop things, delay or disrupt them

Power games at work tend to be based around external power, which is open to misuse. For example, the refusal to divulge important information, veiled threats about non-conformity, the unnecessary show of authority. Each is based on self-interest with little regard for others. Often those concerned don't realize that others see through their games; they are so self-interested that they don't register others' reactions. The first step in de-escalation is to spell out to the protagonist the behaviours that you are witnessing and the effects on other people. It's more difficult for them to play power games when you make it clear that you can see right through them and will continue to observe them.

The transactional analysis model says that we operate from three different 'ego states':

Adult ego-state

In this state, I think, feel and behave in response to what is happening around me right now and I use all the resources available to me as a fully grown-up person

Parent ego-state

In this state, I think, feel and behave in ways which copy my parents or parent figures

Child ego-state

In this state, I think, feel and behave in ways which I used as a child

The psychological model, transactional analysis, suggests that we behave from three basic states, labelled *parent*, *adult* and *child*. The person acting like a parent expects a childlike response from others. When someone else does behave like a child (for example, cowed or scared of the person playing the power game) it continues to reinforce the power play. Speak like an adult to the power player – calmly, rationally and factually – and encourage anyone who has been subjected to the power play to do the same.

Here's a simple example: the power player snaps 'Go and close that door!' The victim of the power play either rushes to close the door (scared child) or snaps back 'Close it yourself!' (petulant child). Reaction one reinforces the sense of power; reaction two creates friction by overtly challenging the power. Neither works. Try calmly saying 'Yes, it is a little cold in here, isn't it? We'd be probably be warmer with the door closed' (adult). Don't volunteer to close it!

The power player who doesn't get the desired reaction will tend to go and play somewhere else.

Models of conflict resolution
Thomas-Kilmann

Kenneth Thomas and Ralph Kilmann contend that there are five basic conflict handling 'modes':

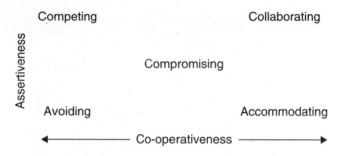

These modes are based on two parameters – assertiveness and co-operativeness. They describe assertiveness as the extent to which someone tries to satisfy their own concerns and co-operativeness as the extent to which someone tries to satisfy the other person's concerns.

In the diagram:

Medium assertiveness + medium co-operativeness (give a little, take a little) = Compromising

Low assertiveness + low co-operativeness (give nothing, take nothing) = Avoiding

Low assertiveness + high co-operativeness (take nothing, give a lot) = Accommodating

Low co-operativeness and high assertiveness (give nothing, take a lot) = Competing

High co-operativeness and high assertiveness (give and take equally) = Collaborating

An understanding of the model can help you to devise useful strategies to resolve conflict at work. Each 'mode' can be very useful if you apply it appropriately. Let's look at their uses. I've written it as though you are one of the protagonists in the conflict so you can see more easily what you may gain or lose with each approach, and you can adapt it for use with your staff:

Mode	Use
Accommodating	When you are wrong (and have the humility to say so) When the issue is less important to you than to the other person When you want to build up credit for later use When the competition is stronger than you When you need to keep the peace

Mode	Use
Avoiding	When it's not as important as other issues facing you When you can't see how the issue can be resolved When it's important for people to cool down When you need time to gather more information rather than trying to resolve something immediately When others can reach a better solution
Compromising	When the goals are only of moderate importance and you can devote your energies more usefully elsewhere When you and your opponent are equally matched with opposing views When you need to create a temporary solution to more complex issues When you are under time pressure to get a result As a fallback position if you cannot collaborate
Competing	In an emergency When a solution is vital, even if it is unpopular On vital issues when you are convinced that you are right When you need to protect yourself against those who would take advantage of you When the door can safely be closed on further discussion/ negotiation
Collaborating	When you need a solution which satisfies both parties equally When you want to gain commitment from everyone involved When you need to move beyond emotional constraints which have hampered the discussions When you want to create a platform on which to build in the future When you want to draw together disparate strands of feeling/ideas/beliefs into a cohesive solution

Use this table to establish the best strategy for the conflict you or others are facing and work towards the goals implied in the 'uses' column.

To achieve your intended outcome in resolving conflict, it is useful to understand the basics of negotiation.

A framework for negotiation

Old-fashioned models of negotiation talk about achieving a 'win-win', but the implication is that the negotiation is some kind of fight and there may be losers. If you enter into a negotiation looking to win, you may display aggressive behaviours which are not helpful in reaching a useful solution. A far better approach is to think of negotiation as collaborative problem-solving. 'You have an issue, I have an issue, so let's work together to see how we can best resolve it.' This isn't about fighting a battle, but about working together for mutual benefit.

Before you negotiate, either on your own behalf or on someone else's, consider the following model which will help you to ask the right questions before and during the negotiation and frame your thoughts so you bring structure to the discussions:

Ideal	What's the perfect outcome? If I could get exactly what I want from this negotiation, what would it be?
Realistic	Realistically, what can I expect to get from this negotiation which would still satisfy my requirements, even if it isn't perfect?
Best alternative	What creative alternative solution would satisfy both me and the other parties involved?

Before a negotiation, determine the 'IRB' for you and for the other party. You will have to make some informed guesses about the IRB for the other side and the framework will help you to focus on the most important information.

It's worth noting that the I and R components will tend to be measured in the same way, and the B component either in a partially or totally different way. Imagine, for example, that you were negotiating a pay settlement between a unionized group of lorry drivers and their directors. The drivers have asked for a 7% increase and the Finance Director has let slip that she may be willing to offer 2.5%.

	Drivers	Directors
Ideal	7%	0%
Realistic	4.75%	2.5%
Best alternative	?	?

The Ideal for the drivers is a 7% increase. The Ideal for the directors is 0% because they probably don't want to increase their salary bills. Realistically, the directors will have to pay at least 2.5% because they have already let slip that this is their offer. **R**ealistically, the drivers can expect that if they negotiate well, the final agreement will be somewhere between 2.5% and 7%. We have now exhausted all possibilities of agreement around salary, so the **B**est alternative must be something other than purely salary. It might, for example, be a smaller salary increase and a change in working conditions (overtime, sick pay, holidays, working hours). The **B**est alternative gives you a chance to be creative and can often steer the conversation away from emotionally charged areas into calmer waters. Use the IRB framework in combination with the Thomas-Kilmann model and you have some great tools for conflict resolution.

DESC model of assertiveness

It's important when resolving conflict to listen hard to each party involved and give them an opportunity to speak. The DESC model offers a nice structure for just that. If you are mediating between two people in conflict, explain the structure and invite each to use it to speak uninterrupted.

Instruct each of the parties to speak matter-of-factly and honestly, refraining from any personal attacks but genuinely expressing their feelings about the situation.

Describe the situation	State exactly what you see as the cause of the conflict. For example: 'Sandra – recently I have been working on a complex project and have needed quiet time when I can really focus. Each time I have started to work, you have interrupted me with questions which I believe you could have answered for yourself. I have politely explained my need to focus, and yet you have continued to talk to me. This is making it impossible for me to get on with my work.'
Express your feelings	'I feel really frustrated. I like you and I don't want to hurt your feelings, but I can't work effectively when you keep talking to me and I feel rude asking you to be quiet!'
Specify what you want	'I would really appreciate it if you would allow me a few hours each day when I can work uninterrupted.'
Consequences	'If you were to do that, it would help me enormously, and I think it would preserve a working relationship which has been good for so long that I would hate to see it damaged as a result of this.'

The benefits of this approach are many:

- It allows individuals to express their emotion without an outburst and without provoking an argument
- It gives permission to each person involved to say what they really think
- It allows them to speak without interruption, which is terribly difficult in an unmediated discussion
- It allows them to set out exactly what they want and explain rationally why that is important to them

Just as you can combine the Thomas-Kilmann model with the IRB negotiation framework, so you can incorporate the DESC model into your discussions.

A model of persuasion and influence

Managing difficult people is about helping them to see alternatives to their reactive or chosen behaviour. Part of the art of resolving conflict is to persuade and influence, presenting attractive alternatives to the current flawed situation. In persuading, we can either appeal to the heart (emotional thought) or head (rational thought). We can effectively 'pull' people towards an alternative way of thinking, or 'push' them in that direction. The combination of these four possibilities gives us a nice model to consider the best approaches to persuasion and influence:

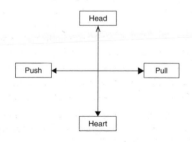

It's unlikely that a single approach will work – you have to be flexible, listening to what others are saying and quickly adapting to them.

Let's see how each approach might work:

- **Head/Push:** 'You know the rules – it's important that if this team is to work properly, we all follow them. Please do this or you know I will have no choice but to take disciplinary action.'
- **Head/Pull:** 'I do think that if you followed the rules, you would find this a more harmonious place to work.'
- **Heart/Push:** 'Come on now! You don't want to be the only one who doesn't join in?'
- **Heart/Pull:** 'Just imagine what fun it's going to be when we all work together on this.'

Cultural aspects of conflict

Culture provides a lens through which we see the world. A group of people who share similar values, beliefs, ideas and ideals will behave differently from those who see everything through a different lens. Any organization may have some semblance of overarching culture and a number of sub-cultures defined through department or specialization, between different age groups, between traditionalists and modernists – between any two groups who see the world and the work differently. In multi-ethnic organizations we add another dimension.

In general terms cultural divides float just below the surface and only rise to the top when one group antagonizes another or when there are intolerable or unresolved differences between the cultural norms and behaviours of different groups.

As a successful manager of others you need to develop cultural fluency: an alertness to cultural differences, a sensitivity to and tolerance of those differences and impartiality in dealing with conflict which arises out of cultural differences.

Here are some key cultural differences which you may encounter at work:

Cultural norm and characteristics	
Universalism Universalists like laws, rules and generalizations. It gives them comfort to know that a guiding rule is in place	**Particularism** Particularists are comfortable with exceptions to rules, evaluating the context in which something happens, rather than applying a universal rule to it
Specificity The preference here is to define everything explicitly, analyse everything and look for measurable results in everything	**Diffuseness** The preference here is to look for patterns and connections, favour both the big picture and process over outcome
Inner direction The inner directed person favours people who strive to realize their conscious purpose	**Outer direction** The outer directed person sees virtue as external – in nature, beauty and human relationships rather than the fulfilment of purpose
Synchronous time Time is cyclical and many things can be achieved at the same time	**Sequential time** Time is a line moving in a single direction. Tasks are completed in sequence. Time is described as wasted, spent, running out.
High-context communication High-context communicators believe that most of a message is conveyed by the context which surrounds it, rather than having to be described explicitly in words. Physical location, the way things are said and shared understandings can be relied upon to give meaning to a communication. To the low-context communicator the apparent lack of clarity in the communication, which relies on non-verbal cues and signals, increases the possibilities of miscommunication because much of the intended message is left unstated.	**Low-context communication** Low-context communication emphasizes directness rather than any reliance on the context as a part of the communication. Verbal communication must be very specific and literal. To the high-context communicator, this may be seen as too direct and confrontational and may escalate conflict.

A quick glance at these polar opposite cultural characteristics will reveal many possible sources of conflict:

Universalists see Particularists as lawless and disorganized	**Particularists** see Universalists as lacking the ability to think freely and too hidebound by rules and regulations
Specificity cultures see Diffuse cultures as too abstract in their thinking, seeing the wood but not the trees	**Diffuse cultures** see Specificity cultures as too detailed, seeing the trees but never appreciating the wood
Those who are **inner directed** may appear over-ambitious and self-centred	Those who are **outer directed** may appear vague and lacking personal drive
Synchronous time thinkers frustrate sequential time thinkers by doing too many things at once and apparently lacking focus	**Sequential time thinkers** frustrate synchronous time thinkers by constantly rushing and appearing to lack spontaneity
High-context communicators are often offended by the directness of low-context communicators	**Low-context communicators** are frustrated by the seeming inability of high-context communicators to get to the point and express themselves clearly

Whilst many of the characteristics described here apply generally to specific national cultures, many of these opposing traits can be seen in individuals within a national culture. When you are involved in resolving conflict listen carefully to what the protagonists say and they will often reveal these traits in their thinking. Once you detect opposing traits you can start to find mutually agreeable solutions.

Summary

No matter how upbeat, caring and supportive you are as a manager, you will encounter conflict at work. Perhaps we should see conflict as a natural outgrowth of diversity which is to be welcomed, but it can be as destructive as it is natural. In managing difficult people in times of conflict, seek out the underlying causes and the potential gains for the individuals involved. Seek support from others when you encounter bullying and act as quickly as you can to prevent its escalation. Notice the type of power that someone is abusing when they play power games and it becomes far easier to counter it. Use the Thomas-Kilmann model, combined with the IRB framework and DESC model to develop a strategy for dealing with conflict and be flexible as you move between push/pull and heart/head in influencing the protagonists of conflict to change their behaviours. Be aware that clashes of culture can cause conflict and determine the underlying differences before applying the other tools and models to reach a solution.

SUNDAY
MONDAY
TUESDAY
WEDNESDAY
THURSDAY
FRIDAY
SATURDAY

Fact-check (answers at the back)

1 Conflict:
a) Is a necessary and inevitable part of working life ❑
b) Is completely unnecessary and avoidable ❑
c) Is a morale booster ❑
d) Is a bar to creativity and competition ❑

2 When things are tense:
a) Show the perpetrators no respect – they don't deserve any ❑
b) Tell the perpetrators to get on with their work and stop playing silly games ❑
c) Allow the perpetrators to attack each other verbally to clear the air ❑
d) Show each party respect and listen to them ❑

3 The four major types of bullying are:
a) Physical attack; undermining personally; isolation; overwork ❑
b) Undermining professionally; sending unpleasant emails; isolation; overwork ❑
c) Undermining professionally; undermining personally; playing practical jokes; overwork ❑
d) Undermining professionally; undermining personally; isolation; overwork ❑

4 Two of the most often abused types of external power are:
a) Legitimate; physical ❑
b) Coercive; directive ❑
c) Expert; participative ❑
d) Connection; information ❑

5 When someone displays, in transactional analysis terms, parent behaviour they expect which response?
a) adult ❑
b) parent ❑
c) child ❑
d) relative ❑

6 Someone high in assertiveness and low in co-operativeness is said to be:
a) avoiding ❑
b) competing ❑
c) accommodating ❑
d) collaborating ❑

7 A better approach to negotiation than 'win-win' is:
a) Ideal, realistic, best alternative ❑
b) Realistic, ideal, alternative choice ❑
c) Ideal, best choice, realistic ❑
d) Ideal, better, best ❑

8 The DESC model of assertiveness is used:
a) To give parties in conflict a platform for an argument ❑
b) To give parties in conflict a bit of peace from each other ❑
c) To give parties in conflict a chance to state their cases ❑
d) To give parties in conflict a public forum ❑

9 Conflict may arise between Universalists and Particularists because:

a) Universalists cannot understand Particularists' desire to adhere to rules ❏

b) Universalists cannot understand Particularists' dislike of regulations ❏

c) Universalists cannot understand Particularists' need for regulations ❏

d) Universalists cannot understand Particularists' failure to adhere to rules ❏

10 High-context communicators:

a) Are as happy with non-verbal cues as with the words spoken ❏

b) Are unhappy with non-verbal cues, favouring explicit statements ❏

c) Are unhappy with shared understandings as an intrinsic part of the message ❏

d) Are as happy with direct and literal communication as with non-verbal cues ❏

SATURDAY

Getting support and escalating issues

It's the final day and if you have worked diligently through each chapter so far, you already have a great selection of tools and techniques to manage difficult people at work. For the most part you will be able to apply these tools alone and resolve most difficult situations. Sometimes, though, a problem just doesn't go away despite your best ministrations.

There is an old adage which says 'If you always do what you always did, you'll always get what you always got – so if you want to get something different you have to do something different'. Well you did everything you could and it still wasn't enough.

You may seek support from your peers, and we'll see how this may work in practice. Sometimes a fresh perspective can be illuminating. Perhaps you will consider asking for help from your own boss.

If difficult behaviour persists and all your other attempts to change it have failed, then you must escalate the issue through more formal channels, perhaps invoking a disciplinary procedure. We'll explore the standard stages in disciplinary proceedings and some general guiding principles for you before and throughout those proceedings. Each organization and, indeed, each country may handle disciplinary issues in subtly different ways. The guiding principles offered here come from UK practice and are similar in many European countries. I strongly recommend that you research your own organization's policies and national variations. If in doubt, seek assistance from the experts in your HR department.

It's easy to feel that somehow you have failed if you are unable to resolve a problem without help. In fact, it takes more courage to ask for help than to battle on alone and others will often be flattered that you turned to them for support and had faith in their ability to help you. If you are starting to worry unduly about how to deal with a difficult person or worse, losing sleep over it, then do ask for support from a peer or from your boss. A problem shared really is a problem halved.

Getting peer support

You've tried everything and nothing has worked. Your difficult person remains difficult. Perhaps the issue is not sufficiently serious for you to invoke disciplinary proceedings but remains sufficiently serious for you to need support in resolving it.

Your peer group can be a fantastic source of support and can offer solutions which you may not have considered. The biggest issue here is confidentiality. As managers we often 'ring-fence' our team, protecting them from criticism by others in the organization and dealing with difficult matters within the team itself. It can feel very uncomfortable talking to 'outsiders' about issues relating to individual team members. You may have some sense that you have failed or that you are talking out of turn. Set these feelings to one side, because you need help and support at this point. Avoid naming names: it may be that your colleague can guess who you are talking about but it is best not to confirm it, so that you can treat the person as a 'case' rather than personalizing the discussion.

Ask your colleague for help. Find somewhere private where you will not be overheard and set out the issue as factually as you can. Ask your colleague if you can explain in detail what has happened so far without interruption, so that you can give the complete picture. Talk through what has happened in sequence so that your colleague has the whole chronology of the misconduct/misbehaviour and your attempts to rectify it. Then encourage your colleague to question you. Stick to the facts as far as possible and avoid saying anything derogatory about the employee in question. Don't rush your colleague – indeed, don't demand an immediate solution, but give them time to consider everything you have said before they suggest alternative actions. Don't dismiss their suggestions out of hand if you can't immediately see the sense in them. Remember that your own actions to date have not worked and sometimes another person can offer insight and ideas which will work where yours failed. At the very least there may be the germ of an idea in your colleague's suggestions.

If you have put your colleague's suggestions into practice and are still struggling to resolve your issue, you may consider talking to your boss.

Getting support from your boss

If going to a colleague felt in any way like an admission of failure then going to your boss may heighten that feeling. Again, set that to one side. In any organization we play complementary roles and should be able to escalate problems which we can't resolve alone. Be careful if you do go to your boss that things have not got out of hand first. You don't want your boss to say 'Why didn't you come and see me sooner?' Your boss may also feel a little insecure faced with a growing problem in the department which he/she is hearing about for the first time. If the issue becomes known to a wider circle in the organization it may undermine your boss.

Assuming that your timing is good and your problem has reached receptive ears, it may be that your boss can exercise some authority which you cannot, directly tackling the errant employee and resolving the issue through legitimate power. At least you will feel supported and sharing the problem with your boss may be a great relief to you.

If the issue is still not resolved, it's time to escalate it to a more formal level – the disciplinary procedure. The good news is that your boss is fully aware of the issue by now and can offer you additional support through the disciplinary process.

Guiding principles on disciplinary issues

You must be seen, as a manager, to have been fair and reasonable at every stage leading to the disciplinary hearing:

- It should be clear that you gave the employee reasonable time to amend their conduct before taking disciplinary action
- You should also have agreed reasonable goals or targets with the employee; your role as a manager is to set people up for success and not for failure
- Ensure that you have complete documentation of each meeting with the employee and of each agreement made regarding the work or behaviours in contention. A primary cause of the failure of disciplinary hearings is lack of documented evidence; then the meeting simply becomes an argument about who said what and to whom
- Ensure that a reasonable investigation takes place into the alleged employee misconduct:
  - In the UK, the ACAS code on grievance and disciplinary procedures will help you to conduct it properly. Ask your HR department for a copy of this or your own local/national guidance
- The investigation should be quick but thorough – it is unfair to keep the employee (and indeed, you) waiting unnecessarily

- The investigation should include, where appropriate, an interview with the employee to hear and document their side of the events leading to the meeting
- The person carrying out the investigation should not be connected to the facts which have given rise to the disciplinary charge
- Consideration should be given to whether the employee should remain in work or be temporarily suspended during the investigation
- Witness statements should be collected
- All documentary evidence of the way you have handled the alleged misconduct should be collated

In the UK, the employee has the right to be accompanied by one other person at the meeting, but custom and practice or the organization's own policies may not allow this. In UK law the companion must be allowed to address the meeting to put the worker's case, summarize it and respond on behalf of the worker to views expressed at the meeting. The companion may also confer with the employee during the meeting but may not answer questions on behalf of the employee, address the meeting if the employee does not wish it, nor prevent the employer explaining their own case.

Stages in disciplinary proceedings

If you decide to take disciplinary action against someone, it's important to know that your HR department does not run the proceedings for you. Their role is to give advice and support and to ensure that everything works according to national and organizational guidelines.

Typical steps in the proceedings are as follows:

● *Establish the facts of the case* (see the previous section about the investigation)

● *A letter to the employee* setting out the nature of the issue: if it is determined that there is a disciplinary case to answer, the employee must be notified of this in writing. The letter should contain sufficient information about the alleged misconduct or poor performance and its possible consequences to enable the employee to prepare to answer the case at a disciplinary meeting. It is normally appropriate to provide copies of written evidence, which may include witness statements, with the notification so that the employee has the same information as the employer. The letter should provide the time, date and venue for the meeting and advise of the right to be accompanied.

● *A meeting to discuss the issue*: at the meeting the employer should explain the complaint against the employee and work through the evidence. The employee should be allowed to set out their case and answer the allegations. The employee should also be given a reasonable opportunity to ask questions, present evidence and call appropriate witnesses. They should also be given the chance to raise points about information provided by witnesses. An employer or employee who intends to call relevant witnesses should give advance notice that they intend to do so.

● *A disciplinary decision*: After the meeting, decide whether or not disciplinary/other action is justified and inform the employee in writing. It's usual to send the employee a written warning where misconduct is confirmed or performance is deemed unsatisfactory. Further misconduct or failure to improve performance within a specified period normally results in a final written warning. If the first misconduct or unsatisfactory performance is sufficiently serious (e.g. where the employee's actions had, or may have, a serious or damaging impact on the organization) the employer may move directly to a final written warning. A first or final written warning must set out the nature of the misconduct/poor performance and the required change in behaviour or required performance improvement, with reasonable timescales. The employee will be told how long the warning is to remain current and will be informed of the consequences of further misconduct, or failure to improve performance, within the specified period following a final warning. Acts of gross misconduct may call for dismissal without notice for a first offence. If an employee is persistently unable or unwilling to attend a disciplinary meeting without reasonable cause the employer may make a decision based on the available evidence.

- *A chance to appeal the decision*: If the employee believes that the decision is unjust they can appeal against it. The appeal should be heard without unnecessary delay and at a mutually agreed time and place. The employee should set out the grounds for the appeal in writing. Ideally the appeal should be heard by a manager with no involvement in the original case. The worker has a statutory right to accompaniment at the appeal and should be informed of the outcome of the appeal as soon as possible afterwards.

You'll notice that throughout the entire proceedings the focus is on fairness. There is no sense that the proceedings favour either the employee or the employer but allow each party the opportunity to state their case before a decision is made. HR can help you to understand and prepare for each stage. Whilst we hope that things never reach this level, provided that you are fair and reasonable, have documented everything at each stage, have given the employee reasonable, agreed goals and time to improve, the proceedings should be relatively straightforward.

Summary

If a problem with a difficult person persists and your own efforts to resolve it have failed, consider involving others. If nothing else it will make you feel supported and others may be able to offer a fresh perspective. First port of call may be a trusted colleague. Ensure that you don't name the difficult employee and try to talk as factually and unemotionally as possible, setting out the details chronologically. Give your colleague time to consider before offering solutions.

If the colleague's ideas don't work or you would prefer to escalate the issue, talk to your boss, being careful not to leave it too late before you do so, so that you don't undermine your boss or present a problem which they could have resolved much earlier on your behalf.

If all else fails, you may have no choice but to invoke disciplinary proceedings. These will vary between organizations and countries and you should seek guidance from your HR department on the correct protocols. You will be expected to show

SUNDAY
MONDAY
TUESDAY
WEDNESDAY
THURSDAY
FRIDAY
SATURDAY

that you were fair and reasonable in goal setting and in giving the employee time to improve, and you should be able to produce comprehensive documentation of the actions that you have taken.

Fact-check (answers at the back)

1 If you always do what you always did:
a) You'll get exactly what you deserve ❏
b) You'll always get what you always got ❏
c) You'll always get something unexpected ❏
d) You'll always get something new ❏

2 Asking for peer support:
a) Can bring a fresh perspective to a difficult situation ❏
b) Is a sign of failure ❏
c) Is dangerous ❏
d) Will reinforce what you had already decided for yourself ❏

3 If you are involved in disciplinary proceedings:
a) You must be seen to have a good case to argue ❏
b) You must be seen to have pushed the employee beyond reason ❏
c) You must be seen to be a hero amongst your peer group ❏
d) You must be seen to be fair and reasonable ❏

4 The UK grievance and disciplinary procedures are published by:
a) ATOS ❏
b) AMEC ❏
c) ACAS ❏
d) ADHD ❏

5 Whoever investigates alleged employee misconduct:
a) Should have close connections to you as the person bringing the charge ❏
b) Should have close connections to the employee facing the charge ❏
c) Should not be connected to the facts which gave rise to the charge ❏
d) Should focus more on opinions than facts during the investigation ❏

6 The person facing disciplinary proceedings:
a) Has no right to attend the meeting but must send a representative instead ❏
b) Has the right to be accompanied by an unlimited number of people at the meeting ❏
c) Has no right to be accompanied at the meeting ❏
d) Has the right to be accompanied by one other person at the meeting ❏

7 In disciplinary proceedings a letter is sent to the employee:
a) Setting out the nature of the issue, possible consequences, time, date and venue ❏
b) Setting out your grievance against them and its likely consequences ❏
c) Setting out the time, date and location of the meeting ❏
d) Setting out the likely outcome of the meeting ❏

8 On receiving notification of the outcome of the disciplinary meeting:
a) The employee has no right to appeal ❏
b) The employee has the right to appeal ❏
c) The employee must appeal ❏
d) The employee must simply abide by the actions noted in the letter ❏

9 If you have been unable to resolve the issue alone or with colleague support:
a) You should implement disciplinary proceedings immediately ❏
b) You should consider yourself an abject failure ❏
c) You may find it useful to talk to your boss ❏
d) You should ask the rest of the team to support you against the difficult employee ❏

10 You are more likely to get a fair result from a disciplinary meeting if:
a) You have been fair and reasonable, documented everything, set reasonable goals and given time for improvement ❏
b) You have argued your case so well that there is no room for dissent ❏
c) You have exaggerated some of your claims about the employee ❏
d) You have asked a friend to investigate on your behalf before the meeting ❏

SUNDAY

MONDAY

TUESDAY

WEDNESDAY

THURSDAY

FRIDAY

SATURDAY

Surviving in tough times

In times of economic recession, people feel under enormous pressure to defend themselves and their jobs, whilst feeling equal pressure to perform at a higher level to prove themselves. An inevitable side-effect is difficult behaviour as stresses build and tempers flare. Cliques form, there may be antipathy towards you, people can become quite tribal and their reactions may appear out of proportion to the events which triggered them.

There is much you can do as a manager to help people through difficult times, both in preventing difficult behaviour and supporting your team. Here are some key ideas:

1 Resist the urge to judge people

It's all too easy to judge others when we don't like their behaviour and to make assumptions about the causes of that behaviour. *Most* people don't deliberately misbehave, and the least we can do when we see someone behaving badly is to support them and try to discover the underlying causes so that we can help them.

2 Maintain a boundary between you and the difficult person

There is an art to displaying empathy and keeping your distance. Let the difficult person know that you understand their issues and will do your best to be supportive. At the same time, keep a little professional distance between you and them. Empathy and sympathy are different and it is important that you do not become emotionally embroiled in someone else's problems. Maintain a professional boundary whilst doing everything you can to help.

3 Stop, think and act

Faced with difficult behaviour, we will often simply react and later regret our reaction. Instead, learn to stop, think, consider the outcomes, and then act, even though everything inside screams out to react in the moment. Your thought-through, considered response will yield dividends.

4 Listen – really listen

For many of us, good listening is the least developed of our communication skills and yet it is the most valuable. You can show no greater sign of respect than to listen to someone and when people feel undermined and under pressure, they may lose self-respect. Be observant and seek out those who appear unhappy and listen to their concerns. You don't necessarily have to find solutions but show your support by listening.

5 Focus on the future

You have no crystal ball and you can't predict the future. You can, however, focus on the future and help your team to do the same. It's highly motivating to have a goal in sight so work with your team to set and achieve goals to lift their morale.

6 Learn to relax

When people around you are unhappy and stressed, it's all too easy to be dragged down with them, yet as a manager you need to demonstrate resilience and positivity even in the face of adversity. Find something to do outside work which is relaxing and healthy, pay attention to your diet and get a good, long sleep each night. If you can learn to relax outside work you'll be a more effective manager in work.

7 Speak positively to your staff and colleagues

We've seen the power of positive language in influencing people. There's a good body of evidence that in workplaces where managers are very positive, the workforce tends to be happier and more motivated. Our starting point in this book was prevention of difficult behaviours and your positive attitude can do much to help your staff to feel better at work. Motivated staff display fewer difficult behaviours.

8 Don't take things personally

If someone displays unwarranted behaviour because they are stressed or miserable, it's not about you! You are not the specific target of their difficult behaviour, just a witness to it. As such, perhaps you can set aside your natural reaction to the behaviour and feel some sympathy for the individual who may be going through tough times. Be supportive whilst keeping a suitable managerial distance, let them know that your door is open and that they can come and talk to you any time. Above all, don't react as though their behaviour is about you.

9 Be aware of survivor guilt

When workmates are made redundant, the survivors can often feel a deep sense of guilt. They know that they have been lucky to survive the redundancies and yet it can make them feel very uncomfortable. It may not be necessary to address this issue directly unless someone particularly wants to talk about it, but it is worth considering as one of the causes of stress which may lead to difficult behaviour.

10 Give your team control when they feel out of control

In difficult times your staff may feel a lack of direction, purpose, status and confidence. Give them back a sense of self-worth through assignment of special responsibilities (which are manageable to someone stressed yet still afford them some increased status), interesting and challenging work which gives them a sense of purpose and direction, and offer them plenty of support so that they achieve their goals and so regain their confidence.

Answers to questions

Sunday: 1a; 2c; 3d; 4b; 5b; 6a; 7c; 8d; 9b; 10d

Monday: 1d; 2a; 3a; 4c; 5b; 6d; 7b; 8c; 9c; 10d

Tuesday: 1b; 2c; 3a; 4d; 5a; 6b; 7d; 8c; 9d; 10a

Wednesday: 1c; 2a; 3b; 4d; 5b; 6c; 7c; 8d; 9b; 10d

Thursday: 1b; 2d; 3a; 4c; 5d; 6c; 7d; 8c; 9a; 10b

Friday: 1a; 2d; 3d; 4d; 5c; 6b; 7a; 8c; 9d; 10a

Saturday: 1b; 2a; 3d; 4c; 5c; 6d; 7a; 8b; 9c; 10a

Notes

ALSO AVAILABLE IN THE 'IN A WEEK' SERIES

BODY LANGUAGE FOR MANAGEMENT • BOOKKEEPING AND ACCOUNTING • CUSTOMER CARE • DEALING WITH DIFFICULT PEOPLE • EMOTIONAL INTELLIGENCE • FINANCE FOR NON-FINANCIAL MANAGERS • INTRODUCING MANAGEMENT • MANAGING YOUR BOSS • MARKET RESEARCH • NEURO-LINGUISTIC PROGRAMMING • OUTSTANDING CREATIVITY • PLANNING YOUR CAREER • SPEED READING • SUCCEEDING AT INTERVIEWS • SUCCESSFUL APPRAISALS • SUCCESSFUL ASSERTIVENESS • SUCCESSFUL BUSINESS PLANS • SUCCESSFUL CHANGE MANAGEMENT • SUCCESSFUL COACHING • SUCCESSFUL COPYWRITING • SUCCESSFUL CVS • SUCCESSFUL INTERVIEWING

For information about other titles in the series, please visit
www.inaweek.co.uk

ALSO AVAILABLE IN THE 'IN A WEEK' SERIES

SUCCESSFUL JOB APPLICATIONS • SUCCESSFUL JOB HUNTING
• SUCCESSFUL KEY ACCOUNT MANAGEMENT • SUCCESSFUL LEADERSHIP
• SUCCESSFUL MARKETING • SUCCESSFUL MARKETING PLANS
• SUCCESSFUL MEETINGS • SUCCESSFUL MEMORY TECHNIQUES
• SUCCESSFUL MENTORING • SUCCESSFUL NEGOTIATING • SUCCESSFUL
NETWORKING • SUCCESSFUL PEOPLE SKILLS • SUCCESSFUL
PRESENTING • SUCCESSFUL PROJECT MANAGEMENT • SUCCESSFUL
PSYCHOMETRIC TESTING • SUCCESSFUL PUBLIC RELATIONS •
SUCCESSFUL RECRUITMENT • SUCCESSFUL SELLING • SUCCESSFUL
STRATEGY • SUCCESSFUL TIME MANAGEMENT • TACKLING INTERVIEW
QUESTIONS

For information about other titles
in the series, please visit
www.inaweek.co.uk

LEARN IN A WEEK
WHAT THE EXPERTS
LEARN IN A LIFETIME

For information about other titles
in the series, please visit
www.inaweek.co.uk